Micah, Nahum

The Turning of the Hourglass

Micah, Nahum

The Turning of the Hourglass

Dr. Bo Wagner

Word of His Mouth Publishers
Mooresboro, NC

All Scripture quotations are taken from the **King James Version** of the Bible.

ISBN: 978-1-941039-67-0
Printed in the United States of America

Word of His Mouth Publishers
Mooresboro, NC
www.wordofhismouth.com

Table of Contents

Introduction

No one (save a few stalwart prophets) in either Israel or Judah ever imagined that time would run out on their kingdoms. In like manner, far away to the northeast, the growing kingdom of Assyria, and to the east, the growing kingdom of Babylon, also vainly imagined that they would take the world and then live forever.

Far above them all, though, beyond the moon, the sun, the stars, and the physical universe itself, God sat, as it were, with a divine hourglass in His hand. It took a mere flick of His wrist to send both Israel and Judah's sands tumbling into the abyss of captivity in Assyria and Babylon.

It would later take another mere flick of the wrist to send the sands of Assyria and Babylon forever into the abyss, while His people flowed home.

Micah

Chapter One
An Incurable Wound

Micah 1:1 *The word of the LORD that came to Micah the Morasthite in the days of Jotham, Ahaz, and Hezekiah, kings of Judah, which he saw concerning Samaria and Jerusalem.* **2** *Hear, all ye people; hearken, O earth, and all that therein is: and let the Lord GOD be witness against you, the Lord from his holy temple.* **3** *For, behold, the LORD cometh forth out of his place, and will come down, and tread upon the high places of the earth.* **4** *And the mountains shall be molten under him, and the valleys shall be cleft, as wax before the fire, and as the waters that are poured down a steep place.* **5** *For the transgression of Jacob is all this, and for the sins of the house of Israel. What is the transgression of Jacob? is it not Samaria? and what are the high places of Judah? are they not Jerusalem?* **6** *Therefore I will make Samaria as an heap of the field, and as plantings of a vineyard: and I will pour down the stones thereof into the valley, and I will discover the foundations thereof.* **7** *And all the graven images thereof shall be beaten to pieces, and all the hires thereof shall be burned with the fire, and all the idols thereof will I lay desolate: for she gathered it of the hire of an harlot, and they shall return to the hire of an harlot.* **8** *Therefore I will wail and howl, I will go stripped and naked: I will make a wailing like the dragons, and mourning as the owls.* **9** *For her wound is incurable; for it is come unto Judah; he is come unto the gate of my people, even to Jerusalem.* **10** *Declare ye it not at Gath, weep ye not at all: in the* *house of Aphrah roll thyself in the dust.* **11** *Pass ye away, thou inhabitant of Saphir, having thy shame naked: the inhabitant of Zaanan came not forth in the mourning of Bethezel; he shall receive of you his standing.* **12** *For the inhabitant of Maroth waited carefully for good: but evil came down from the LORD unto the gate of Jerusalem.* **13** *O thou inhabitant of Lachish, bind the chariot to the swift beast: she is the beginning of the sin to the daughter of Zion: for the transgressions of Israel were found in thee.* **14** *Therefore shalt thou give presents to Moreshethgath: the houses of Achzib shall be a lie to the kings of Israel.* **15** *Yet will I bring an heir unto thee, O inhabitant of Mareshah: he shall come unto Adullam the glory of Israel.* **16** *Make thee bald, and poll thee for thy delicate children; enlarge thy baldness as the eagle; for they are gone into captivity from thee.*

The background of the messenger

Micah 1:1 *The word of the LORD that came to Micah the Morasthite in the days of Jotham, Ahaz, and Hezekiah, kings of Judah, which he saw concerning Samaria and Jerusalem.*

The time period was the latter half of the eighth century BC. So, a bit over eight hundred years before Christ, roughly twenty-eight to twenty-nine hundred years before our day, the Prophet Micah ministered. We do not know much about him, but we do at least know a little. Obviously, we know his name, Micah, which means "Who is like Jehovah?" It was a name that expected a negative response: "No one is like Jehovah!"

Micah was a Morasthite, which means he was from the little town of Moresheth-gath, which was about twenty miles southwest of Jerusalem. He was Judaean by birth, prophesied in Jerusalem, and was a younger contemporary of Isaiah, and also a contemporary of Hosea and Amos. (Feinberg,153).

Micah ministered during the reigns of Jotham, Ahaz, and Hezekiah, which means he knew what it was like to minister on a whiplash-inducing roller coaster of conditions. The first king he ministered under, Jotham, was a good and godly king. The next king he ministered under, Ahaz, the son of Jotham, was one of the absolute worst and most wicked kings the kingdom ever had. The next king he ministered under, Hezekiah, the son of Ahaz, was one of the best and godliest kings the kingdom ever had.

Those three kings reigned for about sixty years in total, and Micah likely ministered during forty to fifty of those years. And, like many other of the minor prophets, he was given a word from God for both Jerusalem and Samaria, representing both the Southern and the Northern Kingdoms. Taken together, Micah and Nahum will show us a divine hourglass, one in which the sands of God's mercy run out with both Judah and Israel and they end up going into captivity, and then God flips everything over and allows the sands of His mercy to slip away from those who took His people captive, as His people come back into their own.

The bringing of the message

Micah 1:2 *Hear, all ye people; hearken, O earth, and all that therein is: and let the Lord GOD be witness against you, the Lord from his holy temple.*

As Micah begins his message, he does so with as expansive a view as is possible. He addresses all the people, tells them to hearken, and then specifies that he means all the people of earth itself. And while commentators like Adam Clarke try to limit this reference to earth merely to Israel, saying that *arets* should be translated as the land, (Clarke,712) that very same word is used in Psalm 24:1 thusly: *The earth* [arets] *is the LORD'S, and the fulness thereof; the world, and they that dwell therein.* So, while *arets* can sometimes be applied in a narrower sense, unless the context clearly limits it, we may simply regard earth as actually meaning earth.

The message God had Micah send out to the whole earth was *let the Lord GOD be witness against you, the Lord from his holy temple.*

This reference to the temple provides yet another question of scope: was this referring to the Temple in Jerusalem, or to God's temple in heaven? Fortunately, we do not have to look far for that answer; the next verse gives it to us:

Micah 1:3 *For, behold, the LORD cometh forth out of his place, and will come down, and tread upon the high places of the earth.*

The temple being referenced, then, is God's abode in Heaven. God intended to be a witness against all the earth (v.2) from that place, that temple, before He came down to them in the judgment He begins to speak of in verse three. As to the judgment itself, it would be severe. Here is the beginning of it in verse three again:

Micah 1:3 *For, behold, the LORD cometh forth out of his place, and will come down, and tread upon the high places of the earth.*

The high places, throughout Scripture, tend to represent much more than merely geographical heights. For the most part, they represented the geographical heights of any area that men would then put their fortresses, palaces, and places of authority upon. So in these words, God was promising to tread on all of those as if they were mere ants and anthills under His feet.

When God speaks of man in terms of ants to His boots, bad things are about to happen.

Micah 1:4 *And the mountains shall be molten under him, and the valleys shall be cleft, as wax before the fire, and as the waters that are poured down a steep place.*

As we arrive in verse four, the God who has threatened the earth now narrows down His focus. Yes, all the earth stands guilty before Him, but there is a particular place and people that grieve Him above all else, and are thus the main target of His wrath:

His people, Israel and Judah. We know this, among other reasons, because the imagery that Micah uses to describe God's coming judgment is imagery that we have seen before, and from a contemporary of Micah, namely Amos:

Amos 9:5 *And the Lord GOD of hosts is he that toucheth the land, and it shall melt, and all that dwell therein shall mourn: and it shall rise up wholly like a flood; and shall be drowned, as by the flood of Egypt.*

As I explained in that place:

> "God did not say that He was going to pick them up and shake them, or pound them into the ground, or throttle them; He simply said that He was going to *touch* the land, with the result being that the land would melt under the judgment.
>
> "What they would see with their eyes would be the Assyrians setting fires left and right, burning and melting everything in sight. What they would not see with their eyes was the God who was reaching out and touching the land to make it all happen." (Wagner, 195)

It means the same from the pen of Micah as it did from the pen of Amos. The land would indeed appear to be melting from the fires and destruction of the Assyrian scourge. Interestingly, that was not the only parallel between these two prophets and passages. Just as God here informed Micah that He would *tread upon the high places of the earth,* He actually showed Amos an example of it happening right then and there:

Amos 9:1 *I saw the Lord standing upon the altar...*

Once again, as I explained there, Amos was prophesying in the Northern Kingdom, Israel. He was right then in Bethel, the place that Amaziah called "The king's chapel and the king's court" in Amos 7:13. So the altar was not the real altar to the real God down south in Jerusalem; the altar God was standing on was the idolatrous altar of the golden calf of Jeroboam.

Both Amos and Micah, then, were seeing or being informed that God was/would stand on/tread on the high places of earth, the centers of power and corruption, and that He would use the coming Assyrian scourge to melt the land.

Micah 1:5 *For the transgression of Jacob is all this, and for the sins of the house of Israel. What is the transgression of Jacob? is it not Samaria? and what are the high places of Judah? are they not Jerusalem?*

The first sentence of verse five will be easy to misunderstand if we do not realize which way it is pointing. If we assume it to be facing forward, we come up with a statement that seems to be incomplete, something like "All of the transgression of Jacob is..." with nothing to finish it, and no listing of the transgressions alluded to. But when we understand that it points backwards, and that *for* is to be taken the way we often take it, "because," the sentence makes perfect sense. It means that the coming judgment of God previously mentioned is for, because of, the transgressions of Jacob and the sins of the house of Israel. That understanding of the first half of the verse also makes perfect sense because Micah goes on in the last half of the verse to begin describing their sins:

What is the transgression of Jacob? is it not Samaria? and what are the high places of Judah? are they not Jerusalem?

The progression of thought, then, runs like this. One, God is going to judge you, Israel. Two, that judgment will be because of your sin. Three, here is that sin.

The sin, as God labels it here, was Samaria in the North and Jerusalem in the South. The two capitals of the two distinct yet related kingdoms were centers of idolatry and iniquity when they should have been centers of the worship of Jehovah and the holy lives that would spring forth from that genuine worship.

Micah 1:6 *Therefore I will make Samaria as an heap of the field, and as plantings of a vineyard: and I will pour down the stones thereof into the valley, and I will discover the foundations thereof.*

Samaria, capital city of the Northern Kingdom of Israel, was situated in a perfect location and perfect soil for a vineyard. It was not a vineyard, though; it was the center of government and power in the North. God, though, was now threatening to reduce it to its most natural usage, that of a vineyard or field for other produce. He was going to wreck it all the way down to the foundations of its precious buildings; those foundations had been covered and unseen for generations; God was going to expose them all. The stones of their buildings would then be tossed off the mountain down into the valley below.

Was God angry at buildings? No, He was angry at what was taking place within those buildings:

Micah 1:7 *And all the graven images thereof shall be beaten to pieces, and all the hires thereof shall be burned with the fire, and all the idols thereof will I lay desolate: for she gathered it of the hire of an harlot, and they shall return to the hire of an harlot.*

Idolatry: it always came back to that. And as was so often the case, those idols and sexual immorality went hand in hand. As Adam Clarke observed of this verse:

"Multitudes of women gave the money they gained by their public prostitution at the temples for the support of the priesthood, the ornamenting of the walls, altars, and images. So that these things, and perhaps several of the images themselves, were literally the hire of the harlots: and God threatens here to deliver all into the hands of enemies who should seize on this wealth, and literally spend it in the same way in which it was acquired; so that 'to the hire of a harlot these things should return.' " (Clarke, 712)

The broken heart of Micah

Micah 1:8 *Therefore I will wail and howl, I will go stripped and naked: I will make a wailing like the dragons, and mourning as the owls.*

Micah was not a disinterested messenger; these were his kin to whom the message of impending judgment was directed. In anguish, then, he proclaims that he will wail and howl, go stripped and naked, make a wailing like the dragons, and a mourning as the owls.

There is obviously a lot to unravel and explain there.

As to the prophet going about stripped and naked in public, that would certainly be frowned on in our day, in which we now have the completed canon of Scripture. We preachers are now messengers with a complete message. But as I have often observed, in their day, the messengers often *were* the message. As such, God often had or allowed prophets to do the seemingly oddest of things so that everyone in the nation would hear about it as it spread person-to-person throughout the land.

Hosea was instructed to marry a prostitute. Ezekiel went into town and lay down on one side of his body for three hundred ninety days, and then switched to the other side of his body for forty days. Micah will now, for some unspecified period of time, go about unclothed, making everyone talk and ask what is going on.

No one will be able to miss him, either; he will not be sneaking quietly, he will wail, howl, be wailing, and make a mourning sound. The two words for wailing are from different words, the first from *sawfad*, and the second from *mispade*. So, the sound of the wailing will not be consistent; it will be changing in tone and tenor as he goes, drawing even more attention.

Howl brings yet another sound into the scene. It is from *yalal*, and it does indeed signify something like a high-pitched howl of anguish. Mourning is from the word *ebel*, and gives the idea of a lower, guttural sound.

His wailing will sound to the people like what they called dragons, which in this case describes creatures that would gather in the night and make horrifying noises. His mourning sounds would be reminiscent of the screech owl. No one was going to miss Micah's demonstration; it would be all anyone was talking about, and for a very long time.

What, though, would bring Micah to do such a thing? The next verse will begin to reveal that for us.

Micah 1:9 *For her wound is incurable; for it is come unto Judah; he is come unto the gate of my people, even to Jerusalem.*

Her wound is incurable; this was the brokenhearted motivation of Micah. As to the identity of this *her* of whom he speaks, we need only to go back to verse seven for that answer, where we find Israel referred to as *she.* It is Israel's wound, therefore, that Micah deems to be incurable; she is dying and does not know she is dying. Her death, though, is not the only damage that Micah foresees. He goes on immediately to say *for it* [meaning the Assyrian invasion] *is come unto Judah; he* [meaning Sennacharib, king of Assyria] *is come unto the gate of my people, even to Jerusalem.*

By prophecy, Micah saw that after Israel fell to Assyria, Sennacherib and Assyria would then turn their attention to the Southern Kingdom of Judah. Not many years later, during the reign of Hezekiah, under whom Micah served, that is exactly what happened:

2 Kings 18:13 *Now in the fourteenth year of king Hezekiah did Sennacherib king of Assyria come up against all the fenced cities of Judah, and took them.*

Things looked bleak indeed for Israel. Here is how far the Assyrians managed to get in their conquest of the Southern Kingdom:

Isaiah 36:1 *Now it came to pass in the fourteenth year of king Hezekiah, that Sennacherib king of Assyria came up against all the defenced cities of Judah, and took them.* **2** *And the king of Assyria sent Rabshakeh from Lachish* <u>*to Jerusalem*</u> *unto king Hezekiah with a great army. And he stood by the conduit of the upper pool in the highway of the fuller's field.*

The Assyrians made it all the way to Jerusalem and besieged it. Here is how near they were to destruction:

Isaiah 8:8 *And he shall pass through Judah; he shall overflow and go over, he shall reach even to the neck; and the stretching out of his wings shall fill the breadth of thy land, O Immanuel.*

In our modern vernacular, Assyria had its hand wrapped around Judah's throat. Only a miracle from God in 2 Kings 19:35 saved them from destruction, and Micah seems not to have been made aware that would happen, at least not yet.

Micah 1:10 *Declare ye it not at Gath, weep ye not at all: in the house of Aphrah roll thyself in the dust.*

Micah, howling, mourning, wailing Micah, now tells his people not to publish the coming calamity of the land down in Gath. Gath was one of the most important cities of the Philistines, the ancient, inveterate enemies of Israel. Weeping among themselves was utterly appropriate, in Micah's view; spreading the news down to Gath, where the reaction would be rejoicing over Israel's fall, though, was something that he could not stomach.

Aphrah is not nearly as familiar to the average peruser of Scripture. It is mentioned only once by that name in Scripture, in the verse we are now considering in Micah. Eight other times, though, it is found as Ophrah. It was a town in the territory of Benjamin, and its full name was Beth-Aphrah or Beth-Ophrah, meaning the house of dust.

It is not hard, then, to see the play on words in the verse. Micah is telling them to roll themselves in dust in the house of dust. Matthew Henry observes of this that people in conditions of great mourning often coated themselves in dust to show their anguish. (Henry, 1306)

Picture it then, as Micah would be wandering about naked, wailing, and commanding others to cover themselves in dust. And, as is the case in so many of the minor prophets, the picture would have seemed all the odder because the kingdom was in one of its more prosperous times in the days of Micah. Because of this, it seemed that none but the prophet could see past the glitter of the day to the gathering clouds in the far North.

Micah 1:11 *Pass ye away, thou inhabitant of Saphir, having thy shame naked: the inhabitant of Zaanan came not forth in the mourning of Bethezel; he shall receive of you his standing.*

Micah now continues mentioning names that may seem obscure to us, but were quite familiar to his hearers of the day. He here addresses the inhabitants of Saphir. Saphir is mentioned by this name only once in Scripture. It was a village amidst the hills of Judah, between Eleutheropolis and Ascalon, and took its name from the Hebrew word for beauty. (Jamieson et al., 588).

This would be another bit of a play on words, as we see his message to them. Micah directed his attention to them and said *Pass ye away, thou inhabitant of Saphir, having thy shame naked.* He was not using the phrase pass away in the sense of dying, as we normally do. It was in much more of a literal sense, and referred to them passing away out of the land as they went away into captivity into Assyria. The play on words is that their beauty would be gone; they would be naked and shamed as they were taken from their homeland.

Two more obscure names are given to us in the last part of the verse, *the inhabitant of Zaanan came not forth in the mourning of Bethezel; he shall receive of you his standing.*

Continuing his usage of plays on words, Micah now mentions the inhabitants of Zaanan, saying that they came not forth in the mourning of Bethezel. Zanaan appears only this once by this name in Scripture, but elsewhere it is referred to as Zenan, and it was a town in the tribe of Judah. A particular way that it is written gives the idea of *coming forth.* (Jamieson et al., 588). And yet, Zaanan/Zenan would not come forth in the time of Bethezel's mourning, the time when they were wrecked by Assyria. The reason they would not come is that they themselves would be in the same predicament.

As to Bethezel, it was also a town in Judah, and it means *the house of narrowing.* It was very near to Zanaan, the town that could not come to help. And as a further indicator of why they could not come to help, Micah says *he* [the Assyrian army] *shall receive of you his standing* [He will gain a foothold in your own property].

Zanaan would not be able to help remove the Assyrians from Bethezel because they would have their own Assyrians to deal with right in their own rapidly narrowing front yards.

Micah 1:12 *For the inhabitant of Maroth waited carefully for good: but evil came down from the LORD unto the gate of Jerusalem.*

Maroth was a small town in the lowlands of Judah. Its name, similar to that chosen by Naomi, Mara, meant bitterness. And yet, the people of Maroth would be waiting expectantly for good to come to them, specifically help from Jerusalem against the Assyrians who would overrun them. Instead, they would, with bitterness, realize that Jerusalem could not help them, and that evil from the LORD had instead made its way to the very gates of the capital city from whence they had hoped for help.

Micah 1:13 *O thou inhabitant of Lachish, bind the chariot to the swift beast: she is the beginning of the sin to the daughter of Zion: for the transgressions of Israel were found in thee.*

Micah now comes to Lachish. This city is mentioned far more frequently in Scripture than the others, and was far more prominent and important. It was a strong city and served as a hub for military and commercial dealings between Egypt and Canaan, later Egypt and Israel. It was also in the tribe of Judah, but was on the very border of the Southern and Northern Kingdoms. Because of its strategic importance, when Assyria invaded, they quickly came after Lachish, conquered it, and made it their center of operations in the land:

2 Kings 18:14 *And Hezekiah king of Judah sent to the king of Assyria to Lachish, saying, I have offended; return from me: that which thou puttest on me will I bear. And the king of Assyria appointed unto Hezekiah king of Judah three hundred talents of silver and thirty talents of gold.*

2 Kings 18:17 *And the king of Assyria sent Tartan and Rabsaris and Rabshakeh from Lachish to king Hezekiah with a great host against Jerusalem. And they went up and came to Jerusalem. And when they were come up, they came and stood by the conduit of the upper pool, which is in the highway of the fuller's field.*

As Micah looked into the future and saw all of this, he said *O thou inhabitant of Lachish, bind the chariot to the swift beast.* In other words, get your fastest means of transportation ready; you are going to be fleeing for your lives. And here is why God made that determination against her: *she is the beginning of the sin to the daughter of Zion: for the transgressions of Israel were found in thee.*

Lachish was the first territory in the Southern Kingdom to buy into the idolatry of the Northern Kingdom and bring it into Judah. When God went searching, He found the sin of Israel in the houses of Lachish. They should have stayed separate and pure; instead, they drank deeply from the cup of Northern wickedness and handed it to their neighbors for them to do the same.

Micah 1:14 *Therefore shalt thou give presents to Moreshethgath: the houses of Achzib shall be a lie to the kings of Israel.*

Of all the words he had spoken thus far, these were perhaps the bitterest to the taste of Micah. Moreshethgath was not just another place to him; it was his own hometown. Its name was normally just Moresheth, but for a time it fell to the Philistines of Gath, and thereafter was often called Moreshethgath. Lachish, whom Micah had just addressed, would one day be reduced to trying to buy help from the residents of Moreshethgath, a far less prominent place, a place only mentioned this single time in the Bible. And if Lachish were so reduced, Moreshethgath itself would also surely fall.

In the last half of verse fourteen, Micah utilizes another play on words, saying, *the houses of Achzib shall be a lie to the kings of Israel.* Achzib was a town on the sea coast, North of Carmel. Its name meant *lying and deceit.* So, Israel, flailing about for help against Assyria, would reach out to the far-flung town of Achzib, and it seems that the result would be a message of "We are on the way with men and arms!" while instead, they gathered their people in, shut their own gates, and left others to fend for themselves.

Micah 1:15 *Yet will I bring an heir unto thee, O inhabitant of Mareshah: he shall come unto Adullam the glory of Israel.*

Mareshah was another way to say the name of Micah's hometown, Moresheth. Its name meant an heir, or heirship. Thus, we find Micah using yet another play on words: he tells the city of heirs that an heir was coming unto them. Only this heir would be the king of Assyria, and it was them, the inhabitants of Mareshah, that he would be inheriting.

From there, He would make his way fourteen miles further southeast to Adullam. That name should sound familiar to any student of Scripture; this was the place of caves and strongholds that David fled to when running from Saul and eventually had hundreds of other men sheltered there with him. For Adullum, this glorious stronghold, to fall, would be a sign that the kingdom was well nigh hopeless.

Micah 1:16 *Make thee bald, and poll thee for thy delicate children; enlarge thy baldness as the eagle; for they are gone into captivity from thee.*

As Micah closes out chapter one of his prophecy, he speaks to the people of the land as a whole, telling them to shave off their hair [poll thee] to the point of absolute baldness, appearing as bald as what we refer to as a bald eagle. This was always a sign of the greatest grief:

Job 1:20a *Then Job arose, and rent his mantle, and shaved his head...*

Why would they want to shave their heads like that? In Micah's words, *Make thee bald, and poll thee for thy delicate children; enlarge thy baldness as the eagle; for they are gone into captivity from thee.*

Their delicate children, innocent tykes who had nothing to do with the sin that led to the destruction, would bear the brunt of the sins of their parents. If they, the hard-hearted people of God, could mourn for nothing else, surely they could at least bring themselves to mourn for this.

Sixteen verses, and not a glimmer of hope in Micah 1; Israel's wound, at least, was incurable. So as things stood at this, the beginning of his prophecy, the sands were slipping out of the hourglass both in Israel and in Judah.

It would have been much wiser for everyone involved to have never behaved in a way that led God to put them on the clock to begin with.

Chapter Two
You Devise, I Devise

Micah 2:1 *Woe to them that devise iniquity, and work evil upon their beds! when the morning is light, they practise it, because it is in the power of their hand.* **2** *And they covet fields, and take them by violence; and houses, and take them away: so they oppress a man and his house, even a man and his heritage.* **3** *Therefore thus saith the LORD; Behold, against this family do I devise an evil, from which ye shall not remove your necks; neither shall ye go haughtily: for this time is evil.* **4** *In that day shall one take up a parable against you, and lament with a doleful lamentation, and say, We be utterly spoiled: he hath changed the portion of my people: how hath he removed it from me! turning away he hath divided our fields.* **5** *Therefore thou shalt have none that shall cast a cord by lot in the congregation of the LORD.* **6** *Prophesy ye not, say they to them that prophesy: they shall not prophesy to them, that they shall not take shame.* **7** *O thou that art named the house of Jacob, is the spirit of the LORD straitened? are these his doings? do not my words do good to him that walketh uprightly?* **8** *Even of late my people is risen up as an enemy: ye pull off the robe with the garment from them that pass by securely as men averse from war.* **9** *The women of my people have ye cast out from their pleasant houses; from their children have ye taken away my glory for ever.* **10** *Arise ye, and depart; for this is not your rest: because it is polluted, it shall destroy you, even with a sore destruction.* **11** *If a man walking in the spirit and falsehood* *do lie, saying, I will prophesy unto thee of wine and of strong drink; he shall even be the prophet of this people.* **12** *I will surely assemble, O Jacob, all of thee; I will surely gather the remnant of Israel; I will put them together as the sheep of Bozrah, as the flock in the midst of their fold: they shall make great noise by reason of the multitude of men.* **13** *The breaker is come up before them: they have broken up, and have passed through the gate, and are gone out by it: and their king shall pass before them, and the LORD on the head of them.*

Micah opened his prophecy castigating the Northern and Southern Kingdoms. Of the Northern Kingdom in particular, his evaluation was *her wound is incurable.*

Both kingdoms would be overrun by Assyria.

Israel, the Northern Kingdom, would not survive.

The making of plans

Micah 2:1 *Woe to them that devise iniquity, and work evil upon their beds! when the morning is light, they practise it, because it is in the power of their hand.*

As Micah opens the second chapter of his prophecy, the setting, as it were, is the bedroom. The hour is the night; most people are sleeping. But the people to whom Micah is addressing these words of woe, indicating impending judgment, are not sleeping, though they are in bed. Instead, they are lying awake and thinking of the next day. And while most people who do such things are working their way through the schedule and the list, these people are actually making plans. They are *devising*, in Micah's words.

That which they are so carefully planning is *iniquity.* Their minds are racing, figuring out bigger and better ways to sin. And, adding to that dark and dirty picture, the next phrase says *and work evil upon their beds!* This paints the picture of them visualizing things step-by-step to make sure they have not missed any details.

They are very, very serious about doing wrong.

They have devised it, they have run through it step-by-step in their minds—and then morning comes:

...when the morning is light, they practise it.

So they lie in bed and devise it, they run through it step-by-step, then they wake up and put their plans into practice, they do the iniquity and evil they have been planning.

The last part of the verse gives us the why:

...because it is in the power of their hand.

They do wrong because they can. Jamieson, Fausset, and Brown said, "Might, not right, is what regulates their conduct. Where they can, they commit oppression; where they do not, it is because they cannot." (Jamieson et al., 590) And it is not any old iniquity and evil they so diligently devise, rehearse, and do; it is specifically the oppression of those weaker than themselves:

Micah 2:2 *And they covet fields, and take them by violence; and houses, and take them away: so they oppress a man and his house, even a man and his heritage.*

They break the tenth commandment, and they know they are doing so. They covet what belongs to others, in this case, fields and house, and they take them by violence. They oppress a man and his house/heritage. The land of those in Israel was to stay within the family forever:

Leviticus 25:23 *The land shall not be sold for ever: for the land is mine; for ye are strangers and sojourners with me.*

Numbers 36:7 *So shall not the inheritance of the children of Israel remove from tribe to tribe: for every one of the children of Israel shall keep himself to the inheritance of the tribe of his fathers.*

And yet, Micah looked around and saw the same thing that Ezekiel railed against:

Ezekiel 46:18 *Moreover the prince shall not take of the people's inheritance by oppression, to thrust them out of their possession; but he shall give his sons inheritance out of his own* *possession: that my people be not scattered every man from his possession.*

This is forever the tendency of the powerful and well-connected, whether in government or merely wealthy enough to always get their way. But it was wrong then, and it is still wrong today.

And God will always have something to say about it:

Micah 2:3 *Therefore thus saith the LORD; Behold, against this family do I devise an evil, from which ye shall not remove your necks; neither shall ye go haughtily: for this time is evil.*

You devise; I devise. God uses the exact same word for what they were doing to others to describe what He will do to them.

This family was the nation of Israel. They devised evil against others, so God devised evil against them. They were powerful enough to wreck the weak, so they did; God would send the Assyrians to wreck them, and they would be too weak to do anything about it. Describing this evil He was sending against them, God said, *from which ye shall not remove your necks; neither shall ye go haughtily: for this time is evil.* The picture He was drawing was of an iron yoke that would be placed around their necks as if they were livestock. They would desperately try to break free, but would not be able to do so. The pride with which they had so casually oppressed others would be utterly broken; no more haughtiness would be within them. *This time*, speaking of the time of their coming captivity to Assyria, would indeed be an evil time. And it was so certain of happening that God spoke of this future event as a present reality.

Micah 2:4 *In that day shall one take up a parable against you, and lament with a doleful lamentation, and say, We be utterly spoiled: he hath changed the portion of my people: how hath he removed it from me! turning away he hath divided our fields.*

Continuing to look ahead in time to the day that He would settle the score with Israel, God promised that when that day came, others would take up a parable against Israel, a doleful lamentation as He then described it.

There is an intentional repetition found in these words. The Hebrew phrase for *lament with a doleful lamentation* is *naha, nehi, nihyah,* which means something like "to lament with a lamentation of lamentations." The way this is laid out is supposed to bring to mind a continuous and monotonous wail. (Jamieson et al., 591)

This was a funeral dirge for the nation of Israel. And the content is from *We be utterly spoiled* in verse four all the way through *are these his doings?* in verse seven.

This first portion was *we be utterly spoiled.* And just as I mentioned a moment ago, since this is a funeral dirge, it is intentionally repetitive. Utterly and spoiled both come from the same word, *shawdad*, meaning to be violently treated. *Shawdad shawdad*, in our terms, means something like "We have been violently violated."

This was God's people! And yet, they brought this on themselves. They utterly spoiled others; God would have others utterly spoil them.

The next part was *he hath changed the portion of my people: how hath he removed it from me!* The portion of His people meant their land, their inheritance. God transferred that from them to Assyria; He changed who would possess it for the time. Once again, this well fit the law of sowing and reaping. They had violently taken away the land of others, changing the title deed from the rightful possessors to themselves, so God would violently take away their land, changing the title deed from them to the Assyrians.

The last phrase of verse four, *turning away he hath divided our fields,* was a picture of God turning His back to Israel and looking the Assyrians in the face instead and handing them, the

Assyrians, the fields of the Israelites for them to divide amongst themselves.

Micah 2:5 *Therefore thou shalt have none that shall cast a cord by lot in the congregation of the LORD.*

Casting a cord by a lot was a reference to one of the ways that they determined the specific will of the LORD on things under certain circumstances in Old Testament times. Remember that the mariners in the book of Jonah did the same thing to find out who the problem was in the midst of their storm. The book of Proverbs often speaks of the casting of lots, and how it could cause contentions between the mighty to cease. When applied to issues of land, this was something that would be done in the house of God in the presence of witnesses to determine who had the right to a portion of land. God was promising that this would not happen anymore, simply because they would not be there for it to happen. The Assyrians were going to remove them and take their land for themselves.

The ministry of words

The doleful lamentation, the funeral dirge for Israel, continues in verse six.

Micah 2:6 *Prophesy ye not, say they to them that prophesy: they shall not prophesy to them, that they shall not take shame.*

Let me paraphrase this verse for you to help you understand who is saying what, and what they are saying:

"Don't prophesy," Israel says to those who are prophesying, and because of that, they will no longer prophesy to them, so that they are no longer shamed by the words of the prophets.

Israel did not like what they were hearing from the prophets, so they told them to stop prophesying. The biggest issue, to them, was how bad the preaching made them feel and how dirty it made them look to others. They wanted their feelings to be unbothered and reputations to be unspotted. But they did not want to live right in order to bring that about; they just simply wanted the preachers to stop preaching.

Some years ago, we had a girl in our youth group who was getting into one very serious sin after another. For their part, her mom and dad were very intentionally turning a blind eye to all of it. They did not look, because they did not want to see. But everybody else was seeing. And every time I spoke to them about it, without fail, their response was "We don't want people thinking badly of our little Penelope."

My response would be, "Then do your jobs and make sure little Penelope lives right."

To which they would respond, "We don't want people thinking badly of our little Penelope."

To which I would respond with a blank stare, realizing I was completely wasting my time.

This is exactly what God was going through with Israel.

Micah 2:7a *O thou that art named the house of Jacob, is the spirit of the LORD straitened? are these his doings?*

This is still part of the funeral dirge that others would be singing for Israel. They were asking in song, *is the spirit of the LORD straitened? are these his doings?*

In so many words, the song was asking if God was making Himself small to Israel, refusing to bless and help them as in former times. It was asking if all of this destruction was really His doing, since He used to lavish them with blessings. This was a sad end to a sad song. And it was a sad end that God was going to briefly and pointedly answer:

Micah 2:7b *...do not my words do good to him that walketh uprightly?*

The words of God are either good to people or bad to people based on how they align with them. If you are going *with* His words, they are good and pleasant. If you are going *against* His words, they are grievous.

But in this case, if the cat is being rubbed the wrong way, the cat is the one facing the wrong direction, and things will never get better until he turns around because God is not going to change the direction He is stroking.

The marring of a legacy

Micah 2:8 *Even of late my people is risen up as an enemy: ye pull off the robe with the garment from them that pass by securely as men averse from war.*

In our day, we often start a sentence with the word lately, as in "Lately, I have been very happy." When God uses the words *of late* in this passage, it means the same thing. Actually, to be precise, is a bit more specific than our use of word lately. It is the same word that in other places is translated as *yesterday*. So, when God says *Even of late my people is risen up as an enemy*, understand that it was going on right that very moment. This was not something that was a few weeks ago or a few months ago; it had happened the very day before, and the day before that, and the day before that.

Of whom had they chosen to be enemies? The last half of the verse answers that, saying *ye pull off the robe with the garment from them that pass by securely as men averse from war.* It was their own countrymen with whom they had become enemies, and countrymen who were themselves absolutely set on peace. They were *averse from war*; they had turned away from strife and wanted no part of it. And yet, wicked people of Israel would see their kin who were doing them no harm and rise up against them as if involved in their own private little war and take both their outer and inner garments from them. They were stripping them even of the bare necessities of life. And they were not content just to victimize men, either:

Micah 2:9 *The women of my people have ye cast out from their pleasant houses; from their children have ye taken away my glory for ever.*

The wording of this verse is stark. Evil men were throwing helpless women out of their homes. Those women had children. The result of what those children saw was *from their children have ye taken away my glory for ever.* Those children, seeing what "God's people" did to them, would never think of God the same way again; all glory He would have ever had in their eyes was stolen away by those evil, covetous men. Little wonder, then, that the God who saw them cast women and children out of their homes would then cast them out of theirs:

Micah 2:10 *Arise ye, and depart; for this is not your rest: because it is polluted, it shall destroy you, even with a sore destruction.*

Like it or not, and they surely did not, God was going to compel them to leave their own land that they had so deeply polluted with their iniquity. In fact, the land itself would fight against them, destroying them when they hoped for its protection. This, they should have anticipated; it is exactly what God warned them had happened and would happen before they even set foot in the Promised Land:

Leviticus 18:24 *Defile not ye yourselves in any of these things: for in all these the nations are defiled which I cast out before you:* **25** *And the land is defiled: therefore I do visit the iniquity thereof upon it, and the land itself vomiteth out her inhabitants.*

When your own land vomits you out, you know you have gone grievously wrong. This land was to be their legacy—it ended up being a marred legacy, at best.

The menacing of the flock

You would think that, at some point along the way, a people in Israel's backslidden state would be confronted by many men of God calling them out for their sin and demanding their repentance. But instead, the people made quite sure that, inasmuch as they were able, they had only a particular type of man appointed as their official prophets:

Micah 2:11 *If a man walking in the spirit and falsehood do lie, saying, I will prophesy unto thee of wine and of strong drink; he shall even be the prophet of this people.*

The usage of the lower-case "s" by our translators on *spirit* in this verse is intentional and instructive. In other prominent places in Scripture where walking in the Spirit is the subject, it is in the upper case:

Romans 8:1 *There is therefore now no condemnation to them which are in Christ Jesus, who walk not after the flesh, but after the Spirit.*

The point of what you see in Micah 2:11, then, is that the false prophet is claiming to be walking in the Spirit, but is instead merely engaging in falsehoods and telling lies. And ironically, much like in our own day, this preacher/prophet is prophesying about booze. He is proclaiming both the availability and the suitability of it. He is saying that the Assyrians will not be able to take the land, and therefore, the booze will still flow freely.

You would think a prophet could find a more suitable message, but, since this is the level to which Israel had sunk spiritually, they loved the message and made anyone who gave it their official prophet.

The wolves of Micah's day were not just in sheep's clothing; they were in clerical robes. And they were menacing the flock with their lies. There would come a day, though, a day far into the future, when the Chief Shepherd would take control of His flock.

The miracle of the latter days

Micah 2:12 *I will surely assemble, O Jacob, all of thee; I will surely gather the remnant of Israel; I will put them together as the sheep of Bozrah, as the flock in the midst of their fold: they shall make great noise by reason of the multitude of men.*

The two words that stand out in contradistinction in verse twelve are *all* and *remnant*. Israel was going to become a remnant; Assyria would take them, and most would die then or in captivity later. But of those who survived, and were born to those who survived, God promised to one day assemble all of them into a complete flock.

This would not be a meager flock and meager fare, either; He said *I will put them together as the sheep of Bozrah, as the flock in the midst of their fold.* Bozrah was well-watered and famed for its fine pasturelands. In a setting similar to that, God would put Israel into the midst of their fold, meaning He would make them as safe as if they were utterly enclosed, with He Himself guarding them.

The last phrase of verse twelve, *they shall make great noise by reason of the multitude of men,* lets us know that they will be so numerous that they will be making a great noise, as does a massive crowd of people in a stadium.

None of this has happened in full yet, but it most assuredly will. As the final verse makes clear, this is a prophecy of the latter days:

Micah 2:13 *The breaker is come up before them: they have broken up, and have passed through the gate, and are gone out by it: and their king shall pass before them, and the LORD on the head of them.*

This is the only time the word *breaker* appears in the Old Testament, and it is, in this place, used as a name or descriptive of God. He is the breaker, meaning the one who will break through the walls and bars and barriers that keep them in captivity, and set them free. They would pass through the gates, their king would go before them, and Jehovah would be their head, their ultimate authority.

The king referenced seems to be David:

Hosea 3:5 *Afterward shall the children of Israel return, and seek the LORD their God, and David their king; and shall fear the LORD and his goodness in the latter days.*

All of this, then, though it has had some measure of partial fulfillment through the years, will only find its complete fulfillment during the Millennial Reign of Christ.

They devised evil. God devised judgment. But God is so good, and such a firm rememberer of His promises, that He also devised restoration. He could rightly have left them for dead as a people, but instead, He chose to bring them home and be their Shepherd.

There is no one quite like Him.

Chapter Three
When the Sun Goes Down on the Prophets

Micah 3:1 *And I said, Hear, I pray you, O heads of Jacob,*
and ye princes of the house of Israel; Is it not for you to know
judgment? **2** *Who hate the good, and love the evil; who pluck off*
their skin from off them, and their flesh from off their bones; **3**
Who also eat the flesh of my people, and flay their skin from off
them; and they break their bones, and chop them in pieces, as for
the pot, and as flesh within the caldron. **4** *Then shall they cry unto*
the LORD, but he will not hear them: he will even hide his face
from them at that time, as they have behaved themselves ill in their
doings. **5** *Thus saith the LORD concerning the prophets that make*
my people err, that bite with their teeth, and cry, Peace; and he
that putteth not into their mouths, they even prepare war against
him. **6** *Therefore night shall be unto you, that ye shall not have a*
vision; and it shall be dark unto you, that ye shall not divine; and
the sun shall go down over the prophets, and the day shall be dark
over them. **7** *Then shall the seers be ashamed, and the diviners*
confounded: yea, they shall all cover their lips; for there is no
answer of God. **8** *But truly I am full of power by the spirit of the*
LORD, and of judgment, and of might, to declare unto Jacob his
transgression, and to Israel his sin. **9** *Hear this, I pray you, ye*
heads of the house of Jacob, and princes of the house of Israel,
that abhor judgment, and pervert all equity. **10** *They build up Zion*
with blood, and Jerusalem with iniquity. **11** *The heads thereof*
judge for reward, and the priests thereof teach for hire, and the

prophets thereof divine for money: yet will they lean upon the LORD, and say, Is not the LORD among us? none evil can come upon us. **12** *Therefore shall Zion for your sake be plowed as a field, and Jerusalem shall become heaps, and the mountain of the house as the high places of the forest.*

Micah opened his prophecy castigating the Northern and Southern Kingdoms. Of the Northern Kingdom in particular, his evaluation was *her wound is incurable*. But this was not arbitrary or capricious. As chapter two unveiled for us, God's coming judgment on them was because they lay awake at night thinking of ways to oppress those weaker than themselves, and then woke up every day and did so.

Chapter three will let us know that both their rulers and their prophets were wholly complicit in the entire sordid affair.

And that they were standing there listening while Micah boldly laid into them.

A practical cannibalism

Micah 3:1 *And I said, Hear, I pray you, O heads of Jacob, and ye princes of the house of Israel; Is it not for you to know judgment?*

Throughout the Minor Prophets, while the people of the land themselves are often castigated, you will find a heavy emphasis on the sins and shortcomings of the rulers of the people. And that is as it should be: to whom much is given, much shall be required.

Micah lends himself to that emphasis in this verse. To their faces, he addresses the heads of Jacob and the princes of the house of Israel, the former meaning the patriarchs of families and tribes, and the latter indicating rulers in a judicial sense, such as judges and magistrates. In both cases, those were men who were entrusted with knowing the law of God and accurately applying it within their sphere of influence.

And that is exactly what Micah meant when he asked them, *Is it not for you to know judgment?* In other words, "Is this not your actual job?" Or, as modern wags tend to put it when someone botches something that was their sole responsibility, "You had one job!"

That modern insult could be applied to them with absolute accuracy. Their job was to know the law of God and accurately apply it within their sphere of influence, and they were not doing it. The very ones that people should have been able to look to for protection under the law of God were utterly useless in that matter. In fact, they were actually worse than useless; they were actively harmful:

Micah 3:2 *Who hate the good, and love the evil; who pluck off their skin from off them, and their flesh from off their bones;* **3** *Who also eat the flesh of my people, and flay their skin from off them; and they break their bones, and chop them in pieces, as for the pot, and as flesh within the caldron.*

In verse two, Micah used the words of a contemporary of his, the fellow minor prophet, Amos. Amos put it in command form:

Amos 5:15 *Hate the evil, and love the good...*

Micah said, *Who hate the good, and love the evil.* So, the rulers of their day were doing the exact opposite of what was right in this. They were supposed to hate the evil, and they loved the evil instead. They were supposed to love the good, and they hated the good instead. And they were the people in charge of enforcing the law!

I am just glad it is not at all like that in America... (For those accustomed to missing the obvious, that was sarcasm.)

After accusing them of hating good and loving evil, Micah then made a further and more picturesque accusation against them, saying, *who pluck off their* [The people's] *skin from off them, and their flesh from off their bones; Who also eat the flesh of my people, and flay their skin from off them; and they break their bones, and chop them in pieces, as for the pot, and as flesh within the caldron.*

Micah was painting a picture of the rulers of the people as being shepherds of the flock. But not good shepherds, horrible shepherds. Good shepherds took care of the flock and tended to the flock and loved the flock. These shepherds were killing the flock and skinning the flock and cooking the flock and eating the flock.

The flock, in this analogy, was the children of Israel. Flesh and blood human beings. God's people. The way the rulers were treating them in a legal sense could only be described this way in a culinary sense. These innocent sheep were coming before their judges pleading for help, and the judges were eating them alive instead.

The God of sowing and reaping saw it and knew exactly what to do about it:

Micah 3:4 *Then shall they* [the heads of Jacob, the princes of the house of Israel] *cry unto the LORD, but he will not hear them: he will even hide his face from them at that time, as they have behaved themselves ill in their doings.*

This once more looked ahead to the coming Assyrian scourge. In that day, these heads of the people who had so oppressed their own and been calloused to the pleading cries of those innocent sheep would turn and cry to their Shepherd, the LORD, and the LORD would respond to them with utter indifference, just as they had responded to their sheep.

They had cannibalized their own; God would allow others to devour them.

A prophetic corruption

Micah 3:5 *Thus saith the LORD concerning the prophets that make my people err, that bite with their teeth, and cry, Peace; and he that putteth not into their mouths, they even prepare war against him.*

Having dealt with the government, God will now use Micah to deal with the other and more important people of authority in the land, namely the prophets. These are they who should have been the messengers of God solely for truth but had, instead, in those days sold out for a paltry price and were now peddling lies.

God said that these prophets were men who *make my people err,* [and] *that bite with their teeth, and cry, Peace;*

To put it mildly, the prophets were not supposed to make the people err [*ta-ah*, wander, go astray], ever. The prophets were supposed to make the people walk right and in the right paths. But these corrupt clergy were actively leading the people astray, just like ill-named progressive clergy do in our own day. It is not just that they do not tell all the truth, it is that they actively tell lies.

Micah said that those of his day *bite with their teeth, and cry, Peace.* That is an odd phrase; briefly, it means "who preach peace as long as they can bite with their teeth." (Keil & Delitzsch, 452) In other words, as long as the ministry is putting fattening meals in their mouths, they will have nothing but good things to say and good predictions to make. You give them pound cake, they preach peace.

That meaning is borne out further by the very next phrase, *and he that putteth not into their mouths, they even prepare war against him.* This means that whoever is not helping to stuff their face, that person gets preached against. That person gets prophecies of war bearing down on him and his family, while others get prophecies of peace.

Thus we find that neither magistrates nor ministers were interested in the flock or in truth; both had come together interested only in fattening themselves at the harmful expense of others. Because of their high station, though, God was going to react pointedly to what the prophets were doing:

Micah 3:6 *Therefore night shall be unto you, that ye shall not have a vision; and it shall be dark unto you, that ye shall not* *divine; and the sun shall go down over the prophets, and the day shall be dark over them.*

There is a dark and dramatic picture we find God painting in this verse. The prophets, those who were supposed to be guiding lights to the people, had instead become prophets for profit. Because of that, God said *Therefore night shall be unto you.* In those words of metaphor, please see smiling ministerial wolves in sheep's clothing, prancing about in the bright light of day, flashing corrupt Colgate smiles to those they were leading astray. Suddenly, a shadow begins to race across the land; it is as if an unscheduled, complete, utter eclipse is happening; within minutes, all is dark, and these prophets are scrambling to try and find torches to light their way.

It all meant that God was going to turn the light out on the prophets. Here is what form that darkness would take:

Micah 3:7 *Then shall the seers be ashamed, and the diviners confounded: yea, they shall all cover their lips; for there is no answer of God.*

Seers is another word for prophets. It meant "one who sees visions." But the prophets of Israel were heading for a day when they were shamed seers, men who received absolutely no vision from God. People would look at them, seeking for answers, and find only red, embarrassed faces.

Diviners is a more unique case still. Diviners were of pagan, heathen origin, and God's people were supposed to have nothing to do with them:

Deuteronomy 18:14 *For these nations, which thou shalt possess, hearkened unto observers of times, and unto diviners: but as for thee, the LORD thy God hath not suffered thee so to do.*

A diviner was one who was either connected with or even possessed by a demon who gave them seemingly supernatural information and knowledge:

Acts 16:16 *And it came to pass, as we went to prayer, a certain damsel possessed with a spirit of divination met us, which brought her masters much gain by soothsaying:*

In spite of how wrong it was, Israel had added diviners to their list of corrupt clergy. But when God finally turned the lights off on everyone who claimed to be hearing from God, *the diviners* [would be] *confounded.* Confounded is another word for shamed; just as the God-ordained office of the prophet would be red-faced in the day of calamity, the pagan-borrowed office of the diviner (which often mixed and overlapped with that of the prophet) would be equally red-faced. They would all *cover their lips; for there is no answer of God.*

Covering of the lips, either with hand or cloth, was a sign of shame for men of Israel. Everything about this picture showed a prophetic corruption so deep that God determined to utterly humiliate all of them—a fate worse than death for men used to being universally respected.

A pointed condemnation

Micah had, without fear or favor, ripped the corrupt prophets of Israel to their very faces. Now, he contrasts himself with them:

Micah 3:8 *But truly I am full of power by the spirit of the LORD, and of judgment, and of might, to declare unto Jacob his transgression, and to Israel his sin.*

Was this pride on the part of Micah? Certainly not; this was a very good shepherd stepping up for the sheep against the very bad shepherds who were devouring them.

Micah claimed to be *full of power by the spirit of the LORD, and of judgment, and of might, to declare unto Jacob his transgression, and to Israel his sin.*

Power is from *koach*, and it indicates might, strength, the ability to move great things and do great things. By means of the spirit of the LORD, Micah had become a mighty, powerful prophet, a man with the strength to do great things for God.

Judgment is from *mishpat*, the exact same word used for it in verse one. The thing that the rulers were supposed to know but did not know, Micah, the preacher, was full of.

Might is from *gebuwrah*, and it indicates valor and bravery. Micah had the might, the valor, the bravery to *declare unto Jacob his transgression, and to Israel his sin.* Other prophets feared to do so, lest their grocery supply diminish and they waste away to obesity. Micah had no such issue; he would preach against sin, even if it meant his own starvation.

Micah 3:9 *Hear this, I pray you, ye heads of the house of Jacob, and princes of the house of Israel, that abhor judgment, and pervert all equity.*

To the groups of political leaders he had previously addressed, Micah now addresses this further condemnation. He says that they *abhor judgment, and pervert all equity.*

Remember, please, that they had one job according to verse one: to know judgment. But not only did they not *know* judgment, they actually *abhorred* it. That word [*ta-ab*] means that they found it abominable, absolutely disgusting. The very thought of the "thou shalts" and "thou shalt nots" of God turned their stomachs, much as the Evangelical Lutheran Church in America progressive pastorette who in early 2025 stood in her pulpit and said, "Before we get started, I wanted to just name something too from the reading from Corinthians. You might have noticed that we didn't read one part out loud and that's because it's yikes,..Paul is being kind of a jerk." (Socher)

Lost clergy always despise the commands and corrections of Scripture.

At the end of the verse, Micah said that they *pervert* [*aqash*, twist, distort] *all equity.* Equity is that which is straight, upright, and correct. Whatever was right and straight, they found ways to twist and turn into a wrong.

So, what is it that Micah wanted them to hear? That will begin in verse eleven, but before that, Micah has a further description of them in verse ten:

Micah 3:10 *They build up Zion with blood, and Jerusalem with iniquity.*

At this point, you should remember that Micah's ministry and message was to both kingdoms, not just the Northern:

Micah 1:1 *The word of the LORD that came to Micah the Morasthite in the days of Jotham, Ahaz, and Hezekiah, kings of Judah, which he saw concerning* ***Samaria*** *and* ***Jerusalem****.*

This now becomes important because he has, in thought and message, now turned his focus from Israel to Judah, and it will remain there for the rest of the chapter.

The clout-carrying men Micah spoke of were actively involved in great civic projects; they were building up Zion and Jerusalem. There was just one problem: they were building everything up with blood and iniquity. They were stealing and killing (blood) and bringing in profitable sin establishments (iniquity).

In our area of the Bible belt, we have seen this. The powers that be in Kings Mountain, NC, against the vociferous objections of a huge amount of the citizenry, and with the help of North Carolina legislators, brought in a casino. They did not care about the evil effects; they simply saw dollar signs.

This kind of thing has been happening for a very long time.

Here is what Micah wanted them all to hear:

Micah 3:11 *The heads thereof judge for reward, and the priests thereof teach for hire, and the prophets thereof divine for money: yet will they lean upon the LORD, and say, Is not the LORD among us? none evil can come upon us.*

Notice three synonymous words: reward, hire, money. The heads (the patriarchs of tribes and families) judged for cash, the priests taught for cash, and the prophets divined (which they should not have been involved with anyway) for cash.

Was/is there something wrong with government officials or the clergy being adequately paid? Certainly not; Paul, referring to the Old Testament, covered that quite nicely:

1 Corinthians 9:6 *Or I only and Barnabas, have not we power to forbear working?* **7** *Who goeth a warfare any time at his own charges? who planteth a vineyard, and eateth not of the fruit thereof? or who feedeth a flock, and eateth not of the milk of the flock?* **8** *Say I these things as a man? or saith not the law the same also?* **9** *For it is written in the law of Moses, Thou shalt not muzzle the mouth of the ox that treadeth out the corn. Doth God take care for oxen?* **10** *Or saith he it altogether for our sakes? For our sakes, no doubt, this is written: that he that ploweth should plow in hope; and that he that thresheth in hope should be partaker of his hope.* **11** *If we have sown unto you spiritual things, is it a great thing if we shall reap your carnal things?*

Both Old Testament and New, governors and preachers were to be adequately paid. But being adequately paid as a minister is very different than *ministering for money!* These charlatans were ministering for money; no money, no message. With a real minister, it will be "no money, buckle up, you are getting preached to anyway!"

In spite of the fact that the government and clergy had completely sold out for profit, Micah said, *yet will they lean upon the LORD, and say, Is not the LORD among us? none evil can come upon us.*

Let that one sink in. They were stealing and maiming and devouring people and dabbling in paganism and twisting everything that was good and ministering only for money, yet whenever someone like Micah warned them of judgment to come, they leaned upon the LORD and said, "The LORD is among us! God is so good, and we are so blessed, nothing bad will ever happen to us. We are living like devils, but check out our latest Facebook post where we tell you that life has never been better and we have never been happier or closer to God!"

They would have felt right at home in our day of unrecognizable "believers."

All of this was going to come at a very high price:

Micah 3:12 *Therefore shall Zion for your sake be plowed as a field, and Jerusalem shall become heaps, and the mountain of the house as the high places of the forest.*

Zion was where the Temple was. Jerusalem was the entire capital city around it. The mountain of the house was the mountaintop upon which the Temple stood. For Zion to be plowed as a field and Jerusalem to become as heaps, mounds of ruin, and the mountain top to become like a forest, was the end of the world to the Jews.

The sun was going down on the prophets—and no one else would fare much better.

Chapter Four
The King Is Coming

Micah 4:1 *But in the last days it shall come to pass, that the mountain of the house of the LORD shall be established in the top of the mountains, and it shall be exalted above the hills; and people shall flow unto it.* **2** *And many nations shall come, and say, Come, and let us go up to the mountain of the LORD, and to the house of the God of Jacob; and he will teach us of his ways, and we will walk in his paths: for the law shall go forth of Zion, and the word of the LORD from Jerusalem.* **3** *And he shall judge among many people, and rebuke strong nations afar off; and they shall beat their swords into plowshares, and their spears into pruninghooks: nation shall not lift up a sword against nation, neither shall they learn war any more.* **4** *But they shall sit every man under his vine and under his fig tree; and none shall make them afraid: for the mouth of the LORD of hosts hath spoken it.* **5** *For all people will walk every one in the name of his god, and we will walk in the name of the LORD our God for ever and ever.* **6** *In that day, saith the LORD, will I assemble her that halteth, and I will gather her that is driven out, and her that I have afflicted;* **7** *And I will make her that halted a remnant, and her that was cast far off a strong nation: and the LORD shall reign over them in mount Zion from henceforth, even for ever.* **8** *And thou, O tower of the flock, the strong hold of the daughter of Zion, unto thee shall it come, even the first dominion; the kingdom shall come to the daughter of Jerusalem.* **9** *Now why dost thou cry out aloud? is* *there no king in thee? is thy counsellor perished? for pangs have taken thee as a woman in travail.* **10** *Be in pain, and labour to bring forth, O daughter of Zion, like a woman in travail: for now shalt thou go forth out of the city, and thou shalt dwell in the field, and thou shalt go even to Babylon; there shalt thou be delivered; there the LORD shall redeem thee from the hand of thine enemies.* **11** *Now also many nations are gathered against thee, that say, Let her be defiled, and let our eye look upon Zion.* **12** *But they know not the thoughts of the LORD, neither understand they his counsel: for he shall gather them as the sheaves into the floor.* **13** *Arise and thresh, O daughter of Zion: for I will make thine horn iron, and I will make thy hoofs brass: and thou shalt beat in pieces many people: and I will consecrate their gain unto the LORD, and their substance unto the Lord of the whole earth.*

To put it mildly, God's people had been led (led astray, really) by very poor leaders. From politics to the pulpit, the shepherds had decimated the very sheep they were to be protecting. But there would and will come a day when those sheep would finally be led by the Chief Shepherd, their rightful and forever King.

Jerusalem set right

Micah 4:1 *But in the last days it shall come to pass, that the mountain of the house of the LORD shall be established in the top of the mountains, and it shall be exalted above the hills; and people shall flow unto it.*

One verse earlier, at the close of chapter three, Micah had mentioned of the house of the LORD—it had not been an encouraging mention:

Micah 3:12 *Therefore shall Zion for your sake be plowed as a field, and Jerusalem shall become heaps, and the mountain of the house as the high places of the forest.*

The picture drawn was that of the mountain on which the Temple of God sat being wrecked, lying neglected for years, and being overrun with wild vines and bushes. Where once were worshippers, there would be only wild animals. But God would never leave His house on Earth in such a state forever. As chapter four begins, God through Micah promises that *in the last days it shall come to pass, that the mountain of the house of the LORD shall be established in the top of the mountains.*

The timing has now jumped a great deal; while the devastation described occurred shortly after Micah's day, this promise will be fulfilled in the last days. This is the Millennial Kingdom of Christ that is being spoken of. Nor was Micah the only one to speak of it. Isaiah, his contemporary, also spoke of it in nearly the exact words as found here in Micah 4:1-3:

Isaiah 2:2 *And it shall come to pass in the last days, that the mountain of the LORD'S house shall be established in the top of the mountains, and shall be exalted above the hills; and all nations shall flow unto it.* **3** *And many people shall go and say, Come ye, and let us go up to the mountain of the LORD, to the house of the God of Jacob; and he will teach us of his ways, and we will walk in his paths: for out of Zion shall go forth the law, and the word of the LORD from Jerusalem.* **4** *And he shall judge among the nations, and shall rebuke many people: and they shall beat their swords into plowshares, and their spears into pruninghooks: nation shall not lift up sword against nation, neither shall they learn war any more.*

The location is as certain as the timing. The mountain of the house of the LORD was an unmistakable reference to Jerusalem, which is mentioned by name in verse two. There will be a thousand-year reign of Christ on Earth, and there will be a Temple from which He reigns on the same spot as the old Temple.

That the mountain and house of the LORD would be reestablished would be a comfort to God's people who were facing ruin at the hands of Assyria and Babylon.

That the mountain and house of the LORD would *need* to be reestablished, though, was a crushing blow to God's people who were facing ruin at the hands of Assyria and Babylon. Their generation would lose it all; it would be future generations that regained it.

All of this, though, as does so much of the writings of the Major and Minor Prophets, drives a dagger through the heart of replacement theology. As far as nations go, God will never forsake His promises to Israel, nor will anyone or anything ever replace them.

In that time when all is finally set right in Jerusalem, the impact will be felt around the world:

Micah 4:2 *And many nations shall come, and say, Come, and let us go up to the mountain of the LORD, and to the house of the God of Jacob; and he will teach us of his ways, and we will walk in his paths: for the law shall go forth of Zion, and the word of the LORD from Jerusalem.*

During the Millennial Reign, Jerusalem will finally be what it was always intended to be, the instruction center of the nations. From the days of the founder of the nation, Abraham, God had this to say:

Genesis 12:2 *And I will make of thee a great nation, and I will bless thee, and make thy name great; and thou shalt be a blessing:* **3** *And I will bless them that bless thee, and curse him that curseth thee: and in thee shall all families of the earth be blessed.*

Israel, then, was to be the center of all nations, and all nations were to be evaluated by their treatment of her. She could not, then, be all of that while being isolated, invisible, and non-instructive. Isaiah echoed this truth in Isaiah 49:1, saying *Listen, O isles, unto me; and hearken, ye people, from far...*

Israel generally failed at that task. But during the Millennial Reign, Micah says that the nations will say *Come, and let us go up to the mountain of the LORD, and to the house of the God of Jacob; and he will teach us of his ways, and we will walk in his paths...*

Notice that it will be their idea and their choice. Verse one says that they will *flow* to it; that word is from *nahar*, and it indicates spontaneity (Feinberg, 168). While people in our day have to be pushed and prodded to come to the House of the Lord, while people in Micah's day often had to be pushed and prodded to go to the house of the LORD, in that day, all nations across the globe will be taking planes and boats and other transportation to go there and hear the instruction of God from the mouth of God.

This is the Millennial Reign; why would that even be necessary? The answer is, for those who are already glorified, it will be a joy, not a necessity. But for those who after the Tribulation Period enter the Millennial Reign in their physical bodies, and for those born to them over the next thousand years, such instruction will be absolutely necessary; no one will be able to successfully live under His reign without knowing His ways.

The last part of verse two says, *for the law shall go forth of Zion, and the word of the LORD from Jerusalem.* All of the rule over all of the Earth will originate and culminate in Jerusalem.

Judgment for the nations

Micah 4:3 *And he shall judge among many people, and rebuke strong nations afar off; and they shall beat their swords into plowshares, and their spears into pruninghooks: nation shall not lift up a sword against nation, neither shall they learn war any more.*

He, Jesus, the Messiah/King, will be the judge over all the Earth. While in our day, rulers of nations merely rattle their sabers or issue strongly worded communiques to other nations, He will be the final judge, and will go so far as to *rebuke strong nations afar off.* This pulls back the veil to the future a bit to allow us a glimpse of what will be. During the Millennial Reign, there will still be individual nations around the world, and some of them will be very powerful nations. Christ will not set up a world where nations are done away with; nations were His idea to begin with.

Rather, He will set up a world in which all nations, no matter their strength, must answer to Him.

In our day, in this world in which there are many nations, some greater and some stronger, the result is almost always war; there have indeed been very few periods of human history that have been without it. But during the Millennial Reign, when Christ rules from Jerusalem, things will be very different. Micah says of that time *and they shall beat their swords into plowshares, and their spears into pruninghooks: nation shall not lift up a sword against nation, neither shall they learn war any more.*

For a thousand years, the instruments of war will be melted down and re-forged into instruments of industry and agriculture. For a thousand years, not only will there be no war, there will not even be anyone learning how to make war. It will be a time of absolute peace—not necessarily because rulers want it that way, but because they are given no other choice by the King who sits on the throne.

All of this will provide mankind with a situation he has not been able to have and enjoy since his expulsion from the Garden of Eden:

Micah 4:4 *But they shall sit every man under his vine and under his fig tree; and none shall make them afraid: for the mouth of the LORD of hosts hath spoken it.*

This is a setting of absolute peace, a slow, enjoyable lifestyle in which mankind once again has the time to attend to his plants and watch them grow.

At this point in the text, you need to be able to view the entire setting, or you will not be able to understand how shocking are the words that follow. The setting Micah has described is one of worldwide peace; people have their gardens and are watching them grow, no one is afraid, and all of it is because of the King who is sitting on the throne in Jerusalem.

With that in mind, look at the next verse:

Micah 4:5 *For all people will walk every one in the name of his god, and we will walk in the name of the LORD our God for ever and ever.*

We are still talking about the Millennial Reign. We are still talking about the time when Jesus is visibly ruling from the throne in Jerusalem. We are still talking about the time when, because of Him, all of the Earth is peaceful and no one is afraid. And yet, even in the midst of that utopia on Earth, we find here that the nations of the world will still be embracing their own gods and rejecting the God that they can now visibly see with their eyes, the God who is responsible for everything they are enjoying.

This also explains how, after being released from his thousand years in the bottomless pit, the devil will so quickly and easily be able to raise up a mass of humanity for one final war against God.

During all of the Millennial Reign, Israel, though, for the first time, will be very and permanently different. In contrast to the nations, Israel will be able to truthfully say *and we will walk in the name of the LORD our God for ever and ever.*

What an odd setting the Millennial Reign affords! All of the Jews will finally have accepted Jesus, their Messiah, and will follow Him forever with all of their hearts, finally recognizing Him as their Jehovah. Many of the nations of the world will be coming up to Jerusalem to receive instruction of the Lord. And yet, in spite of all that, there will also be countless multitudes across the world who reject all of that and continue to follow their own gods.

Jeremiah was right when he said *The heart is deceitful above all things, and desperately wicked: who can know it?*

Micah 4:6 *In that day, saith the LORD, will I assemble her that halteth, and I will gather her that is driven out, and her that I have afflicted;* **7** *And I will make her that halted a remnant, and her that was cast far off a strong nation: and the LORD shall reign over them in mount Zion from henceforth, even for ever.*

Having expressed the coming condition of the far-flung nations of the world, in these verses, God turns His attention specifically back to His people, Israel. All of the descriptive terms here apply to Israel and to her near periods of exile and all her future exiles. For those in Micah's day, it was all about being brought back from Assyria (the Northern Kingdom) and Babylon (the Southern Kingdom).

God would cause His people to halt [*tsala*, be made lame]; He would drive her out and afflict her because of her sin. And while Judah had several major returns from captivity to their land, and people here and there from Israel managed to get back to their country, the ultimate fulfillment of verse seven has never come close to being accomplished. It will be in the last days that God *will make her that halted a remnant, and her that was cast far off a strong nation: and the LORD shall reign over them in mount Zion from henceforth, even for ever.*

There is a lovely progression in this multi-layered promise. God made Israel to halt; He made her lame and powerless before her enemies. He would bring her back and change her from a halting people to a remnant people; they would not be as strong and numerous as before, but they would no longer be lame, either. From that remnant, though, God would rebuild them as a strong nation, and then He would go on to *reign over them in mount Zion from henceforth, even for ever.*

Truly, the nations of the world will be radically different when the King sits on the throne.

Jesus arriving

Micah 4:8 *And thou, O tower of the flock, the strong hold of the daughter of Zion, unto thee shall it come, even the first dominion; the kingdom shall come to the daughter of Jerusalem.*

When Micah spoke of the tower of the flock, you need to know that, while this is the first and only time we find these

English words in the Bible, the name/title was actually a very old one by the time of Micah:

Genesis 35:21 *And Israel journeyed, and spread his tent beyond the tower of Edar.*

Tower of the flock in Micah 4:8 is the exact same Hebrew name as the Tower of Edar in Genesis 35:21. It was an actual tower where sheep were kept and guarded, and it was on the outskirts of Bethlehem. So, Micah's prophecy in 4:8 was the same as his prophecy in 5:2, a prophecy of the birth of Jesus. Bethlehem, just five miles or so south of Jerusalem, is described here as the daughter of Zion/Jerusalem.

Micah's prophecy of this place was that *unto thee shall it come, even the first dominion; the kingdom shall come to the daughter of Jerusalem.*

The first dominion does not mean "first, and then there will later be a second, and a third, etc.," it means first as in primary, chief, ultimate. The kingdom came to Bethlehem because the King of kings was born in Bethlehem. Again, Micah will go further in elaboration of this in his very next chapter; just know for now that, having spoken of the King and His Millennial Kingdom, Micah has now dropped back in time to show where and when it will all begin, namely Bethlehem, about 750 years after Micah's own day.

Joy through purging

Micah will now begin to look back from the coming of Christ to the days just shortly future to his own time, specifically the coming Babylonian invasion and captivity. Isaiah also wrote of this in nearly the same words, but the subtle change from the way Isaiah wrote it to the way Micah wrote it lets us know that Isaiah's word likely came first, and Micah's later:

Micah 4:9 *Now why dost thou cry out aloud? is there no king in thee? is thy counsellor perished? for pangs have taken thee as a woman in travail.*

Isaiah 13:8 *And they shall be afraid: pangs and sorrows shall take hold of them; they shall be in pain as a woman that travaileth: they shall be amazed one at another; their faces shall be as flames.*

When Isaiah wrote it, it was *shall.* By the time Micah wrote it, it was *have.* The wickedness of the people had moved it to a level in which a future event was now as certain as a present reality.

Here, again, was the series of questions Micah asked concerning that terrible coming day: *why dost thou cry out aloud? is there no king in thee? is thy counsellor perished? for pangs have taken thee as a woman in travail.*

By way of answer, yes, they had a king and counselors, but they may as well not have. Their kings and counselors were wicked, inept, and useless and did more harm than good. Gone would be the days of giants such as David and Solomon and Hezekiah; Judah would devolve into the weak and dirty hands of men like Jehoahaz, Jehoiakim, Jeconiah, and Zedekiah, and would fall to the Chaldeans.

The next verse spells that part out explicitly:

Micah 4:10 *Be in pain, and labour to bring forth, O daughter of Zion, like a woman in travail: for now shalt thou go forth out of the city, and thou shalt dwell in the field, and thou shalt go even to Babylon; there shalt thou be delivered; there the LORD shall redeem thee from the hand of thine enemies.*

There is much to see in this verse. To begin with, Micah now, for the second time, pictures Judah as a woman going into labor. There is no agony on Earth quite like that; Judah will be screaming in pain and wondering if she will even survive.

Beyond that, though, is the rather remarkable, specific prophecy that it will be Babylon to which she falls rather than Assyria. It was the Assyrians that were the power of the world in the day of Micah, and it was the Assyrians who were already coming against all the land of Israel and Judah. Micah's prophecy would have seemed to make as much sense in that day as someone prophesying that it would be Canada that overran Europe rather than Germany during World War II.

There is no God like the real God, and there is no book at all like the Bible!

Finally, though, is the jaw-dropping assessment that *there* [in Babylon] *shalt thou be delivered; there the LORD shall redeem thee from the hand of thine enemies*.

The Babylonians took them into captivity. The Babylonians were their enemies. And yet, God used those enemies and that captivity to deliver and redeem Judah rather than to destroy her. Their enemies and captivity became used as the very instruments for God saving them from destruction and redeeming them, buying them back for His own.

Even in well-deserved judgment, God would use everything happening to redeem rather than ruin His people.

Micah 4:11 *Now also many nations are gathered against thee, that say, Let her be defiled, and let our eye look upon Zion.*

Micah has now moved in thought and content back to his own day and days shortly to follow. In those very days, there were indeed very many nations gathered against them; Assyria, Edom, other nations of the surrounding areas, all desiring to see them overthrown, all desiring to look at Jerusalem as it was defiled and devastated.

It was not going to turn out well for them:

Micah 4:12 *But they* [the nations gathered against them] *know not the thoughts of the LORD, neither understand they his counsel: for he shall gather them as the sheaves into the floor.*

In verse eleven, we find many nations *gathered* against God's people. In verse twelve, we find that God will *gather* those many gathered nations as sheaves into the threshing floor.

Those nations thought God was giving up His people for their destruction; they did not know the thoughts of the LORD. No anti-Semite knows the thoughts of the LORD.

As for those nations being gathered into the threshing floor, as you may well imagine, that was an ominous reference for them:

Micah 4:13 *Arise and thresh, O daughter of Zion: for I will make thine horn iron, and I will make thy hoofs brass: and thou shalt beat in pieces many people: and I will consecrate their gain unto the LORD, and their substance unto the Lord of the whole earth.*

Both in the days shortly after Micah's and in the years to come, as Israel came back to their land, God would and did let Israel turn and thresh their enemies as wheat on the threshing floor.

That process was often done, as is pictured here, by allowing animals to stomp the sheaves to separate the good from the bad, leaving the bad for destruction. God pictures here His people as those oxen, only with hooves of brass, doing this to the enemies who have come against them. God promised that Israel would beat in pieces many people, and they did exactly that on multiple occasions between the time of Micah and the time of the coming of Christ.

The closing words of this portion of Micah's prophecy was *and I will consecrate their gain unto the LORD, and their substance unto the Lord of the whole earth.*

When Cyrus gave the Jews permission to return to their own land after their years of captivity in Babylon, he gave them back the sacred vessels of the Temple, which Nebuchadnezzar had carried away. In later years, the Maccabees and their successors recovered much of the treasure that neighboring nations had deprived them of, and the treasure taken was devoted to Jehovah. (Clarke, 719)

Micah's prophecy in chapter four was wide-ranging, far-reaching, and often bounced back and forth with hundreds or thousands of years of gaps. But the main thought in them was one that brought Judah comfort then, and still brings any child of God comfort now:

The King is coming.

Chapter Five
From The Manger to the Millennial Reign

Micah 5:1 *Now gather thyself in troops, O daughter of troops: he hath laid siege against us: they shall smite the judge of Israel with a rod upon the cheek.* **2** *But thou, Bethlehem Ephratah, though thou be little among the thousands of Judah, yet out of thee shall he come forth unto me that is to be ruler in Israel; whose goings forth have been from of old, from everlasting.* **3** *Therefore will he give them up, until the time that she which travaileth hath brought forth: then the remnant of his brethren shall return unto the children of Israel.* **4** *And he shall stand and feed in the strength of the LORD, in the majesty of the name of the LORD his God; and they shall abide: for now shall he be great unto the ends of the earth.* **5** *And this man shall be the peace, when the Assyrian shall come into our land: and when he shall tread in our palaces, then shall we raise against him seven shepherds, and eight principal men.* **6** *And they shall waste the land of Assyria with the sword, and the land of Nimrod in the entrances thereof: thus shall he deliver us from the Assyrian, when he cometh into our land, and when he treadeth within our borders.* **7** *And the remnant of Jacob shall be in the midst of many people as a dew from the LORD, as the showers upon the grass, that tarrieth not for man, nor waiteth for the sons of men.* **8** *And the remnant of Jacob shall be among the Gentiles in the midst of many people as a lion among the beasts of the forest, as a young lion among the flocks of sheep: who, if he go through, both treadeth down, and teareth* *in pieces, and none can deliver.* **9** *Thine hand shall be lifted up upon thine adversaries, and all thine enemies shall be cut off.* **10** *And it shall come to pass in that day, saith the LORD, that I will cut off thy horses out of the midst of thee, and I will destroy thy chariots:* **11** *And I will cut off the cities of thy land, and throw down all thy strong holds:* **12** *And I will cut off witchcrafts out of thine hand; and thou shalt have no more soothsayers:* **13** *Thy graven images also will I cut off, and thy standing images out of the midst of thee; and thou shalt no more worship the work of thine hands.* **14** *And I will pluck up thy groves out of the midst of thee: so will I destroy thy cities.* **15** *And I will execute vengeance in anger and fury upon the heathen, such as they have not heard.*

Micah spent three chapters describing the calamities that were to fall both on the Northern and the Southern Kingdoms. But then, in chapter four, he looked ahead in time to when the King would be sitting on the throne in Jerusalem and ruling all nations. Now, here in chapter five, he will come back to the present day, and his focus will be squarely on the Southern Kingdom, Judah, and what she would be facing not too far down the road.

A shock for the present

Micah 5:1 *Now gather thyself in troops, O daughter of troops: he hath laid siege against us: they shall smite the judge of Israel with a rod upon the cheek.*

The opening phrase, *Now gather thyself in troops, O daughter of troops,* is clearly militaristic in its nature. It is Judah and her armies that are being addressed. God is telling them through the prophet to gather together and to prepare for war, because it is coming, whether they like it or not.

The outcome, though, was not in doubt. Speaking of a future event as if it were present certainty, he said *he hath laid siege against us: they shall smite the judge of Israel with a rod upon the cheek.*

He is Nebuchadnezzar and the Chaldeans. While Judah would be rescued by God from the Assyrian siege, a bit more than a century later, they would fall to the Chaldean siege. At that time, they, the Chaldeans, would *smite the judge of Israel with a rod upon the cheek.*

The judge of Israel referred to her king, Zedekiah, and the smiting with a rod upon the cheek was indicative of the greatest humiliation and embarrassment that such a person could ever be put to. And indeed, Zedekiah did experience this in its fullest measure. His own sons were slain before his eyes, and then, to make sure he would never see anything else that could help erase the memory, his own eyes were put out, and he was carried away captive to Babylon, 2 Kings 25:7.

Remember, please, that no one in his day would have believed that any of this was coming. For starters, Micah ministered mostly during a very prosperous and successful time both in Judah and in Israel. Secondly, the scourge of the Earth and the immediate threat of their day was Assyria, not Babylon. And yet, around 150 years later, Micah's words proved to be prophetic and given by God indeed, as they came to pass just as he said.

A Savior for the future

Hearing the dire words of Micah, anyone who believed them would have been devastated and shaken to the core. And yet, Micah's message was not done; there was hope yet to be given.

Micah 5:2 *But thou, Bethlehem Ephratah, though thou be little among the thousands of Judah, yet out of thee shall he come forth unto me that is to be ruler in Israel; whose goings forth have been from of old, from everlasting.*

Micah just got done telling of the day when their king, Zedekiah, would be broken to bits, along with their kingdom. And yet, he now speaks of the time when not *a* king, but *the* King, the long-awaited Messiah, would come to the kingdom. His coming, though, would be geographically from the oddest of places, it would seem.

When Micah was prophesying that the Messiah would come from Bethlehem, he had to specify that he meant Bethlehem/Ephratah, which is the same name as Ephrath, the original name of the town. The reason he had to specify that in his day is because there was actually another town of Bethlehem up in Zebulon's territory.

If Micah had uttered this prophecy during the days of David, favored son of Bethlehem, or Solomon or even Rehoboam, this would not have been necessary; everyone would have known automatically that he was talking about Bethlehem in Judah. But as Micah put pen to parchment to write of the coming Messiah, look at what he said about Bethlehem in his day:

But thou, Bethlehem Ephratah, though thou be little among the thousands of Judah...

Bethlehem had no glory left by the days of Micah. Bethlehem, which had always been sort of small, was now tiny as far as population went. Bethlehem was a city that very much looked like it would not even survive, a city that was well on its way to becoming a ghost town. And yet God had Micah make this prophecy, a prophecy that came to pass perfectly when Jesus first lifted up His tiny voice and cried as He came into the world of man as the sacrifice for that world of men.

Here is how Micah described Him: *whose goings forth have been from of old, from everlasting.*

He would be a babe who created the very universe into which He now came as a babe. He would be one minute old, and utterly ageless and eternal at the exact same moment.

Micah 5:3 *Therefore will he give them up, until the time that she which travaileth hath brought forth: then the remnant of his brethren shall return unto the children of Israel.*

Let us put some names with the pronouns of this verse for explanatory purposes:

Micah 5:3 *Therefore will he* [the Messiah/King of verse two] *give them* [Israel and Judah] *up, until the time that she which travaileth* [Mary, the mother of Jesus the Messiah/King] *hath brought forth: then the remnant of his* [Jesus as a Jew] *brethren shall return unto the children of Israel.*

This verse has two levels, one found in Bethlehem in the time of Christ, and the other found in the Millennial Kingdom Micah spoke of in chapter four. Both Israel and Judah lost their kingdoms during the days of Micah or shortly thereafter. Israel, the Northern Kingdom, never did have a wholesale return. Judah, the Southern Kingdom, had several different returns from her captivity in Babylon. By the time of Christ, though, representatives of all twelve tribes were once again found to be in their land. Ultimately, though, this will not find its complete fulfillment until the Millennial Reign of Christ, when all of the remnants of Israel have been gathered together and are once again one nation and one kingdom under their King.

It is that very view we still see in the next verse:

Micah 5:4 *And he* [the Messiah/King] *shall stand and feed in the strength of the LORD, in the majesty of the name of the LORD his God; and they* [they of the now reunited kingdom of Israel] *shall abide: for now shall he* [Jesus] *be great unto the ends of the earth.*

An important bit of theology that we find in this verse, as in many other places of Scripture, is the separate personages of the Trinity. While Jesus Himself is often referred to as the LORD, meaning Jehovah, here we find Him standing and feeding in the majesty of Jehovah His God. The Father and the Son are one (John 10:30), and the Father is the Son's God (John 20:17) at the exact same time.

During the Millennial Reign, we find that Jesus shall *be great unto the ends of the earth.* There will be no place He is not known, nor anywhere He is not regarded as great, even among those who reject Him.

Micah 5:5 *And this man shall be the peace, when the Assyrian shall come into our land: and when he shall tread in our palaces, then shall we raise against him seven shepherds, and eight principal men.*

As is so often the case with the prophecies of the prophets, things will bounce back and forth in time, sometimes with thousands of years of gaps between them. Such is the case as we enter verse five, for Micah has now come back to his own day, and from the Southern Kingdom back to a view of the Northern Kingdom. He is still seeing Messiah as well, though; He, though not yet even born, is the One referred to in the words *this man shall be the peace.*

Jesus from Heaven was going to do a work on Earth well before He even arrived in the flesh.

Micah reminded the North that *the Assyrian shall come into our land* and *he shall tread in our palaces.* This he has already been warning of, though this is the first place he actually mentions them by name.

The last half of the verse is intriguing: *then shall we raise against him seven shepherds, and eight principal men.*

To begin to unravel who these seven shepherds and eight principal men are, we need to see verses five and six together, because it is one continuous thought between them. I will once again explain pronouns to help you see how the thought runs:

Micah 5:5 *And this man* [Jesus/the Messiah King]*shall be the peace, when the Assyrian shall come into our land: and when he* [the Assyrian] *shall tread in our palaces, then shall we* [Jesus and God the Father] *raise against him* [the Assyrian] *seven shepherds, and eight principal men.* **6** *And they* [the seven shepherds and eight principal men] *shall waste the land of Assyria with the sword, and the land of Nimrod* [meaning Assyria, here, though in other places it refers to Babylon. Nimrod's original kingdom encompassed the territory of both] *in the entrances thereof: thus shall he* [the Chaldeans] *deliver us from the*

Assyrian, when he [the Chaldeans] *cometh into our land, and when he treadeth within our borders.*

There is a lot there, so let's work through it step by step.

One: the Jesus of Bethlehem was the Son of God in Heaven from eternity past, and was active for His people well before the first advent.

Two: the Assyrians would come against Israel and take it, and would then turn their attention to Judah.

Three: the LORD would, at that time, raise an adversary against the Assyrians to deliver His people. This would first come in the form of He Himself miraculously delivering them (2 Kings 19:35), but would go further and:

Four: he would raise against them *seven shepherds, and eight principal men.* Throughout the poetical books and the books of the prophets, the one-number-then-the-next formula was for emphasis. This, then, means that God would raise up a group of powerful men against Assyria. The Chaldean empire fits this description; it was an empire built out of a conglomeration of people, primarily Aramean, Chaldean, and Babylonian, but including other smaller groups as well.

Five: Assyria ruled the world, including Israel, which they conquered in 722 B.C. The Chaldeans later conquered and took all of Assyria's lands, including Israel.

This, then, was a good news/bad news situation. Yes, Assyria, Israel's enemies, would be defeated for good. But Judah would later fall to the very Babylonians who delivered them and others from the Assyrians.

Micah 5:7 *And the remnant of Jacob shall be in the midst of many people as a dew from the LORD, as the showers upon the grass, that tarrieth not for man, nor waiteth for the sons of men.* **8** *And the remnant of Jacob shall be among the Gentiles in the midst of many people as a lion among the beasts of the forest, as a young lion among the flocks of sheep: who, if he go through, both treadeth down, and teareth in pieces, and none can deliver.*

Both verse seven and verse eight start with the same phrase, *And the remnant of Jacob shall be.* Both then follow up with the phrases *in the midst of many people* (v.7) and *among the Gentiles in the midst of many people* (v.8).

These verses, then, apply to the last days, the days when the remnant of Jacob, meaning those brought back into their land to form the kingdom under Jesus, their Messiah, are under much different conditions than the days in which they were overrun by Assyrians and Babylonians. Micah has bounced back to his subject of verse four, the Millennial Reign of Christ.

Since she was founded as a nation, Israel has been many things in the view of the nations of the world—few of them positive. But during the Millennial Reign, verse seven informs us that she will be a blessing among the nations of the world (dew), and verse eight informs us that she will also be feared and respected among the nations of the world (a lion). Anyone vainly imagining that God has forever set aside His people, the Jews, knows nothing of Scripture or of the heartbeat of God.

Micah 5:9 *Thine hand shall be lifted up upon thine adversaries, and all thine enemies shall be cut off.*

Micah, speaking this prophecy to his people, refers to them directly when he says "thine." The people who were being told that they would be overrun by their adversaries in shortly coming days are now being told that their hand would be lifted up upon their adversaries, and that all their enemies would be cut off.

A scouring of the wicked

Micah 5:10 *And it shall come to pass in that day, saith the LORD, that I will cut off thy horses out of the midst of thee, and I will destroy thy chariots:*

Comparing this passage with two other passages from two other prophets, we can quickly figure out who it is that is being addressed in this verse:

Isaiah 2:6 *Therefore thou hast forsaken thy people the house of Jacob, because they be replenished from the east, and are soothsayers like the Philistines, and they please themselves in the children of strangers.* **7** *Their land also is full of silver and gold, neither is there any end of their treasures; their land is also full of horses, neither is there any end of their chariots:* **8** *Their land also is full of idols; they worship the work of their own hands, that which their own fingers have made:*

Zechariah 9:10 *And I will cut off the chariot from Ephraim, and the horse from Jerusalem, and the battle bow shall be cut off: and he shall speak peace unto the heathen: and his dominion shall be from sea even to sea, and from the river even to the ends of the earth.*

It is God's people, the Jews, therefore, that Micah is addressing in verse ten. It is their chariots and horsemen that God is going to be cutting off. But why? The context has been of the latter days, and of them being both a blessing among the nations and a respected people among the nations. Why, then, would God, in that context, say that He was taking away their military might?

Anyone who has read the record of the Jews in the Old Testament should have no trouble figuring this out. They constantly relied on their military might to the exclusion of relying on the LORD. They constantly defied God because they believed they were strong enough to defend themselves.

In the last days, God will remove that foolish notion from them. He will be their defense, and they will rely on Him rather than on their military. They surely need their military now—there will come a day when they do not.

That will not be the extent of God's scouring of His people. Look at the next four verses all at once, and I will highlight the common theme for you:

Micah 5:11 *And I will cut off the cities of thy land, and throw down all thy strong holds:* **12** *And I will cut off witchcrafts out of thine hand; and thou shalt have no more soothsayers:* **13**

Thy graven images also will I *cut off, and thy standing images out of the midst of thee; and thou shalt no more worship the work of thine hands.* **14** *And I will pluck up thy groves out of the midst of thee: so will I destroy thy cities.*

This was God speaking to His people—about Him rescuing them in the latter days! His rescue of His people would start with Him wrecking their military, and He would then go on to cut off their cities, throw down their strongholds, cut off their witchcrafts, cut off their idols, pluck up their groves, and destroy their cities!

God is going to devastate His people to deliver His people. He is going to ruin all of the sinful, fleshly, and carnal things they have relied on. He will take their best efforts to do things on their own and reduce them all to rubble. It will be then, and only then, that He does what comes next:

Micah 5:15 *And I will execute vengeance in anger and fury upon the heathen, such as they have not heard.*

Almost since the time Israel became a nation, they trusted themselves, their power, their intelligence, their ability, to deliver them and make them great. During the Tribulation Period, God will fix that problem once and for all. He will allow them to be wrecked and ruined so that He can then turn and absolutely obliterate their enemies, and they can then, in turn, look to Him, as they should have been doing the entire time.

Isn't that the way it is with us as well, though? How often do we trust our power, our intelligence, our ability, relegating God to little more than an insurance policy in case of an unplanned disaster?

That never went well for Israel, and it will go no better for us.

Look to Him, always, in everything.

Chapter Six
A Blast from the Past

Micah 6:1 *Hear ye now what the LORD saith; Arise, contend thou before the mountains, and let the hills hear thy voice.* **2** *Hear ye, O mountains, the LORD'S controversy, and ye strong foundations of the earth: for the LORD hath a controversy with his people, and he will plead with Israel.* **3** *O my people, what have I done unto thee? and wherein have I wearied thee? testify against me.* **4** *For I brought thee up out of the land of Egypt, and redeemed thee out of the house of servants; and I sent before thee Moses, Aaron, and Miriam.* **5** *O my people, remember now what Balak king of Moab consulted, and what Balaam the son of Beor answered him from Shittim unto Gilgal; that ye may know the righteousness of the LORD.* **6** *Wherewith shall I come before the LORD, and bow myself before the high God? shall I come before him with burnt offerings, with calves of a year old?* **7** *Will the LORD be pleased with thousands of rams, or with ten thousands of rivers of oil? shall I give my firstborn for my transgression, the fruit of my body for the sin of my soul?* **8** *He hath shewed thee, O man, what is good; and what doth the LORD require of thee, but to do justly, and to love mercy, and to walk humbly with thy God?* **9** *The LORD'S voice crieth unto the city, and the man of wisdom shall see thy name: hear ye the rod, and who hath appointed it.* **10** *Are there yet the treasures of wickedness in the house of the wicked, and the scant measure that is abominable?* **11** *Shall I count them pure with the wicked balances, and with the bag of* *deceitful weights?* **12** *For the rich men thereof are full of violence, and the inhabitants thereof have spoken lies, and their tongue is deceitful in their mouth.* **13** *Therefore also will I make thee sick in smiting thee, in making thee desolate because of thy sins.* **14** *Thou shalt eat, but not be satisfied; and thy casting down shall be in the midst of thee; and thou shalt take hold, but shalt not deliver; and that which thou deliverest will I give up to the sword.* **15** *Thou shalt sow, but thou shalt not reap; thou shalt tread the olives, but thou shalt not anoint thee with oil; and sweet wine, but shalt not drink wine.* **16** *For the statutes of Omri are kept, and all the works of the house of Ahab, and ye walk in their counsels; that I should make thee a desolation, and the inhabitants thereof an hissing: therefore ye shall bear the reproach of my people.*

Chapter five of Micah took us from Christ's birth in Bethlehem through the Millennial Reign of Christ. And while much of that was undeniably positive and encouraging, it also pointed to the time when God would ruin Israel to redeem her. Her trust in her idols, strength, and abilities would ultimately have to be broken for God to bring her to the heights of glory He has in store for them.

Chapter six is going to bring Micah and his message back to their present day, back to the Northern Kingdom of Israel—and to a very damaging blast from the past.

A call for testimony

Micah 6:1 *Hear ye now what the LORD saith; Arise, contend thou before the mountains, and let the hills hear thy voice.*

As Micah begins this portion of his prophecy, you need to be able to see the setting in your mind's eye. Remember, then, that he is speaking these words that are now written down for us. He has an audience.

As he addresses that audience, he begins with *Hear ye now what the LORD saith*. He is, then, going to be telling them what

God is saying to them through him. He is, at that moment, God's mouthpiece.

God's message to them is *Arise, contend thou before the mountains, and let the hills hear thy voice.* He is commanding them to stand up, just to begin with. An official proceeding is to take place, and it is to be a legal proceeding; *contend* is from the word *riyb*, and it indicates a lawsuit, of sorts. God is taking them to court, as it were, and they are being summoned to rise and speak. Their jury is to be the mountains all around them. Those hills are being personified as if they were people, people who will decide between the two opposing parties.

After they state their case, though, the opposing party will state His:

Micah 6:2 *Hear ye, O mountains, the LORD'S controversy, and ye strong foundations of the earth: for the LORD hath a controversy with his people, and he will plead with Israel.*

In verse one, we saw the word *contend*, from *riyb*. Now, in verse two, we twice find the word *controversy,* both of which are also from that same word, *riyb*. The people are at legal odds with God, and God is at legal odds with the people.

In verse one, the mountains were to hear the people's side of the story. In verse two, the mountains are to hear God's side of the story.

The final phrase of verse two, *and he will plead with Israel,* bears a bit of explanation in light of how we, in our modern vernacular, view the word *plead.* When we use or hear that word, the picture it brings to mind is of someone whimpering and begging, someone who is weak and helpless.

Nothing could be farther from the meaning of this word in this verse. Remember, please, that this is a legal proceeding being described. In that context, even today, we still use the word "pleading" in the same way Micah used it. It is from the word *yakach*, and it means to prove, decide, judge, and rebuke. It is a term of argumentation and accusation.

When the legal battle is between you and God, and He is set to argue against you, things are not going to go well for you.

Micah now spells out what God is arguing against them:

Micah 6:3 *O my people, what have I done unto thee? and wherein have I wearied thee? testify against me.*

As God begins His argument, He does so in an emotional rather than an academic manner. It is not "Here are the facts of the situation in alphabetical or chronological order," it is *O my people, what have I done unto thee? and wherein have I wearied thee? testify against me.*

In our terms, it means something like "O my people, what have I ever done to you? How have I offended you? Go ahead and testify against Me right now!"

Clearly, the right answer was "nothing, nothing, and we cannot do so." In fact, He had actively and consistently done them nothing but good, and He will remind them of that in the next two verses.

Micah 6:4 *For I brought thee up out of the land of Egypt, and redeemed thee out of the house of servants; and I sent before thee Moses, Aaron, and Miriam.*

God now takes them back to when they first became a free nation. He reminds them that He was the one who brought them out of Egypt to start with; He redeemed them from the house of servants. And while "the house of servants" may not sound so bad, when you understand that servants is from the word *ebed*, you will quickly understand that it was abysmal. You see, the exact same Hebrew phrase used here is used in Exodus 20:1 as well:

Exodus 20:2 *I am the LORD thy God, which have brought thee out of the land of Egypt, out of the house of bondage* [ebed].

The house of servants and the house of bondage are the same thing. Their "service" was that of abject slaves, people to be used up, then thrown away.

God redeemed them from that. Further, He said *I sent before thee Moses, Aaron, and Miriam.* Moses was their deliverer, lawgiver, and leader for forty years. Aaron was their High Priest for forty years. Miriam was a prophetess among them for forty years. God gave them stability of leadership and greatness of leadership all the years that they needed it most.

Their history of blessings from God did not end there:

Micah 6:5 *O my people, remember now what Balak king of Moab consulted, and what Balaam the son of Beor answered him from Shittim unto Gilgal; that ye may know the righteousness of the LORD.*

When Micah said this, it took them back in time to the wilderness wanderings yet again, this time to the events of Numbers 22. Balak, king of Moab, hired a prophet for profit named Balaam to curse Israel for him. Instead, no matter what location Balak took him to view the Children of Israel, God compelled him to utter a blessing on Israel rather than a curse.

Micah told them to remember that, *that ye may know the righteousness of the LORD.* In other words, if had God brought them out of Egypt only to allow them to be cursed and destroyed in the wilderness for no good reason, they may well have seen God as unrighteous. But since God turned Balaam's hoped-for curse into a blessing, since He preserved them from harm just as He promised, they could only rightfully view Him as absolutely righteous.

A contrite heart

Micah 6:6 *Wherewith shall I come before the LORD, and bow myself before the high God? shall I come before him with burnt offerings, with calves of a year old?* **7** *Will the LORD be pleased with thousands of rams, or with ten thousands of rivers of oil? shall I give my firstborn for my transgression, the fruit of my body for the sin of my soul?*

In verses six and seven, Micah is still speaking to the people, but is now doing so in a rather unique manner. He opened the conversation by picturing his audience in a legal setting, at odds with God. Now he speaks as if he is them, answering to the charges.

The first question he puts into their mouths is *Wherewith shall I come before the LORD, and bow myself before the high God? shall I come before him with burnt offerings, with calves of a year old?*

They are asking how they could make things right, and then suggesting what they had in mind. To their thinking, if they bring God burnt offerings and calves of the first year, both of which the law actually called for, all may be well.

Between the words of verses six and seven, though, something within them would recognize that merely observing those called-for sacrifices would never be enough, under the circumstances. In verse seven, then, they expand things exponentially, saying *Will the LORD be pleased with thousands of rams, or with ten thousands of rivers of oil? shall I give my firstborn for my transgression, the fruit of my body for the sin of my soul?*

The hyperbole is evident; the only thing we do not know is whether the words would be viewed as sincere or sarcastic. Were they desperate and willing to do anything? Or were they saying these words with a wink and a nod? Regardless, they were, at least verbally, offering thousands of rams, tens of thousands of rivers full of olive oil, and even their firstborn children to God in order to satisfy the God who was pleading against them.

Having spoken as if he were the people asking the question, Micah now answers the question he has put into their mouths:

Micah 6:8 *He hath shewed thee, O man, what is good; and what doth the LORD require of thee, but to do justly, and to love mercy, and to walk humbly with thy God?*

"You already know," Micah was saying, "You already know what God requires of you. He is not asking for burnt offerings and calves and rams and rivers of oil and for your firstborn children. Here is what He views as good, here is what He requires of you. You are to *do justly, and to love mercy, and to walk humbly with thy God.*"

Three things: God required three things of them in light of their current state.

First, He expected them to do justly. Justly is from *mishpat*, and in this instance, it indicates a fair-handedness in all of their dealings. How were they doing on this? As we have already learned, not well at all. Look back at chapter three, and a previous usage of *mishpat* from Micah:

Micah 3:1 *And I said, Hear, I pray you, O heads of Jacob, and ye princes of the house of Israel; Is it not for you to know judgment* [mishpat]*?* **2** *Who hate the good, and love the evil; who pluck off their skin from off them, and their flesh from off their bones;* **3** *Who also eat the flesh of my people, and flay their skin from off them; and they break their bones, and chop them in pieces, as for the pot, and as flesh within the caldron.*

This requirement of God to the people, then, was not random or haphazard. They were not doing justly; they were doing the exact opposite of justly.

Second, He expected them to love mercy. How were they doing with that? Once again, not well at all:

Micah 2:1 *Woe to them that devise iniquity, and work evil upon their beds! when the morning is light, they practise it, because it is in the power of their hand.* **2** *And they covet fields, and take them by violence; and houses, and take them away: so they oppress a man and his house, even a man and his heritage.*

They had the power to hurt people and take their stuff, so they did so, heedless of the cries for mercy that doubtless rang in their ears.

Third, He expected them to walk humbly with their God. By now, you likely know that, since God brought it up, they were not doing any better in that area than in the first two:

Micah 2:6 *Prophesy ye not, say they to them that prophesy: they shall not prophesy to them, that they shall not take shame.*

The people were so brazen in their pride that they told the prophets to shut up; they were not interested in hearing anything that would embarrass them.

Rivers of oil would never be enough; God wanted something much more valuable, specifically, a contrite heart.

A corruption maintained

Micah 6:9 *The LORD'S voice crieth unto the city, and the man of wisdom shall see thy name: hear ye the rod, and who hath appointed it.*

Micah has ended his illustration of a legal proceeding. Now, he will, over the course of several verses, spell out the root of the iniquity that has brought them to this point.

The words he begins with certainly need some explaining to the modern Western mind. Who is the man of wisdom? How does one see a name? How does one hear a rod?

When the LORD's voice cries to a city in judgment, as God was right then doing, any man of wisdom would see God's name in that pronouncement of judgment. In other words, he would not look at the prophet speaking the words; he would look past the prophet to the God behind the words. In this case, he would not be seeing the name Micah in his mind; he would be seeing the name Jehovah, in whose name Micah was speaking.

As to the hearing of the rod and hearing the one who appointed it, this simply means they would be hearing from God's messenger of the rod of judgment that was coming and would recognize that they were hearing God's words, not man's.

If you have ever uttered the modern figure of speech "Don't shoot the messenger," then you have some sense of the point of this verse.

Micah 6:10 *Are there yet the treasures of wickedness in the house of the wicked, and the scant measure that is abominable?* **11** *Shall I count them pure with the wicked balances, and with the bag of deceitful weights?*

The answer to Micah's question in verse ten was "yes." There were, in fact, *treasures of wickedness in the house of the wicked, and the scant measure that is abominable.*

The treasures of wickedness that Micah was now lambasting referred to the unjust riches that powerful people were amassing by fraud. We begin to see that when Micah references the *scant measure.* A scant measure was a lean scale; it was a scale that weighed something as lighter than it was, so the buyer could purchase it for less than it was worth. God spells that out very specifically in verse eleven when He says *Shall I count them pure with the wicked balances, and with the bag of deceitful weights?*

The picture he paints is of a tricky system whereby you could weigh a product as lighter than it was, and then turn right around and weigh your payment as heavier than it was. It was fraud, and the Children of Israel were masterful at it.

Micah 6:12 *For the rich men thereof are full of violence, and the inhabitants thereof have spoken lies, and their tongue is deceitful in their mouth.*

The rich men of the house of the wicked were full of violence. Their fraud was backed by force; question or cross them, and things would go very badly for you.

The inhabitants of the house of the wicked, the average Joes associating in the wickedness, were as deceitful as their leaders.

Micah 6:13 *Therefore also will I make thee sick in smiting thee, in making thee desolate because of thy sins.*

God was going to smite His people for their sins, and He was going to do so until they were sick. Their violence would bring vexing that led to vomiting.

God said that He would make them desolate; it means they would be wasted and left in ruins. The apple of His eye would be as a core in the gutter by the time His judgment against them ran its course.

Micah 6:14 *Thou shalt eat, but not be satisfied; and thy casting down shall be in the midst of thee; and thou shalt take hold, but shalt not deliver; and that which thou deliverest will I give up to the sword.*

The threatening promise God made in this verse was a very longstanding one. Around a thousand years earlier, God first gave it to them in this form:

Leviticus 26:26 *And when I have broken the staff of your bread, ten women shall bake your bread in one oven, and they shall deliver you your bread again by weight: and ye shall eat, and not be satisfied.*

As Micah observes in verse sixteen, God will use the sword, specifically the sword of the Assyrian, to bring about this famine and hunger. The enemy will take much of what they have, the rest will be eaten bit by bit in the siege until there is no more, and any new stores that they could conceivably come by will be taken by those Assyrians as well. God said, *thy casting down shall be in the midst of thee.* This would not be a hidden thing; it would be in the open, for all of the Children of Israel to see.

Micah 6:15 *Thou shalt sow, but thou shalt not reap; thou shalt tread the olives, but thou shalt not anoint thee with oil; and sweet wine, but shalt not drink wine.*

Once again, Micah paints the picture of people desperately trying to grow things by which they can survive, only to have others tread their olive and take their oil and drink their wine. This would be devastation on a humiliating scale.

All has been bleak so far in this chapter, and devastatingly so. But why? Why would God so savage His own people?

It is in the last verse of chapter six that we come to the specific answer:

Micah 6:16 *For the statutes of Omri are kept, and all the works of the house of Ahab, and ye walk in their counsels; that I should make thee a desolation, and the inhabitants thereof an hissing: therefore ye shall bear the reproach of my people.*

And now we see it. Nearly two centuries later, the wicked laws installed by the sixth king of the North, Omri, were still in place and being followed. Nearly a century and a half later, the evil works of the house of Ahab, the seventh king of the North, were still the guideposts for the kings and people of the North.

Omri and Ahab were the two vilest kings Israel ever had. For Israel to still be wallowing in their filth generations later was inexcusable. This was what led to them not doing justly and not loving mercy and not walking humbly before their God.

Because of this, God determined to make them a desolation, and the inhabitants thereof a hissing, and make them bear the reproach of His people.

Desolation is from *shahmaw*, and it means a horror. Looking at them would be like watching the hapless victims in a monster movie.

Hissing is from *sheraqah*, and it indicates a shrieking. They would be shrieking, and others who saw them would shriek for them.

Reproach is from *kerpah*, and it means scorn, shame, and taunting. God's people, who should have been the jewel of the Earth because of their relationship with the one true God, would instead be the butt of everyone's jokes.

They had more than enough time to make all of this right. Instead, their blast from the past was going to blow up their present.

Chapter Seven
Where Have All the Good Men Gone?

Micah 7:1 *Woe is me! for I am as when they have gathered the summer fruits, as the grapegleanings of the vintage: there is no cluster to eat: my soul desired the firstripe fruit.* **2** *The good man is perished out of the earth: and there is none upright among men: they all lie in wait for blood; they hunt every man his brother with a net.* **3** *That they may do evil with both hands earnestly, the prince asketh, and the judge asketh for a reward; and the great man, he uttereth his mischievous desire: so they wrap it up.* **4** *The best of them is as a brier: the most upright is sharper than a thorn hedge: the day of thy watchmen and thy visitation cometh; now shall be their perplexity.* **5** *Trust ye not in a friend, put ye not confidence in a guide: keep the doors of thy mouth from her that lieth in thy bosom.* **6** *For the son dishonoureth the father, the daughter riseth up against her mother, the daughter in law against her mother in law; a man's enemies are the men of his own house.* **7** *Therefore I will look unto the LORD; I will wait for the God of my salvation: my God will hear me.*

Chapter six of Micah revealed for us a longstanding problem in the Northern Kingdom that was leading them to judgment in the present: they were still walking in the statutes and ways of Omri and Ahab after nearly two centuries. They had more than enough time to change course—they just did not do so. This led to the most horrendous of wickedness by the days of Micah, wickedness that made God determine to send the Assyrians to take His cherished people into captivity.

As Micah begins chapter seven, he seems to do so with all of that in mind, and with a lament that, if there were only some good men left somewhere in the land, perhaps the judgment could be staved off.

The desire of the prophet

Micah 7:1 *Woe is me! for I am as when they have gathered the summer fruits, as the grapegleanings of the vintage: there is no cluster to eat: my soul desired the firstripe fruit.*

Having laid out the wickedness of the people for six chapters and the judgment that is sure to come, Micah now, in a seeming moment of transparency of the heart, opens chapter seven with an emotional outpouring.

"*Woe is me*!" he says in anguish. This phrase is only found seven times in Scripture, and this is the last of those seven. It is a wail, an anguished cry, the pouring forth of a broken heart.

After grabbing everyone's attention with his "*Woe is me*," Micah begins to talk about fruit. He says that he is as a man who is looking around at things after the summer fruits have been gathered and the earliest clusters of the grapes have been taken. These were the early figs and the choicest clusters of grapes; they came early on in the harvest; the quality diminished as the harvest became late in the year. In his analogy, Micah wanted those things, but was compelled to say *there is no cluster to eat: my soul desired the firstripe fruit.*

Picture Micah looking out at bare vines of the vineyard, with maybe just a handful of wrinkled, sub-standard grapes left hanging on them, and looking out at fig trees with all of the very best figs gone, and just a few leftovers that no one would want hanging on the branches.

As you can likely discern, though, Micah was not lamenting an agricultural problem: he was lamenting an anthropological problem.

The deficiency in the land

Micah 7:2 *The good man is perished out of the earth: and there is none upright among men: they all lie in wait for blood; they hunt every man his brother with a net.*

And now we come to the point of Micah's lament in verse one. It is not that Micah cannot find good grapes and suitable figs; it is that he cannot find good men. Just like the firstfruits of the grapes and figs would bring life and cheer to the land, good men would bring God's blessings and favor on the land. But as Micah looked out at Israel, the vineyard/fig tree, he saw nothing but small, sour fruit on her branches.

Gone were the days of giants like David and Solomon; in their place, devils like Ahaz now occupied the once hallowed throne. And for their part, the citizens followed the crown in this corruption; Micah said *there is **none** upright among men: they **all** lie in wait for blood; they hunt **every man** his brother with a net.*

Those universal terms are stark and shocking. Micah deemed that there was not a single upright [*yashar*] man in the land, not a single man who was righteous and straight in his dealings.

He then took that general statement further and said that *they all lie in wait for blood.* It is not merely that they happen upon a chance to kill and rob another; it is that they lie in wait for anyone who comes by their way for that specific purpose.

The next accusation takes things even a step further still, saying *they **hunt** every man his brother with a net.* So, they lie in wait for a while, and if no one is coming by that they can rob and kill, they leave their hiding place, go grab a net, and go hunting for someone close to them, a family member, even, to rob and kill.

With the universal terms Micah applies to these three levels of wickedness, it is no wonder that he began verse two with *The good man is perished out of the earth.*

The depth of the iniquity

Micah 7:3 *That they may do evil with both hands earnestly, the prince asketh, and the judge asketh for a reward; and the great man, he uttereth his mischievous desire: so they wrap it up.*

The phraseology Micah now uses to describe the wicked men of his day is breathtaking: he charges them with doing *evil with both hands earnestly.*

Wrap your thinking around that one. They are not content to do evil merely with a left hand or a right hand, or even the left hand then the right hand in turn. No, they will not be satisfied unless they can have both hands engaged in wickedness at the same time, all the time. And they are not lackadaisical about it; they do so *earnestly.*

They need help to enjoy success with such a massive level of wickedness, though. Look at all of verse three again, and you will see how that help comes about:

That [in order that] *they may do evil with both hands earnestly, the prince asketh, and the judge asketh for a reward; and the great man, he uttereth his mischievous desire: so they wrap it up.*

The first step in all of the wicked men of Micah's day being able to do evil earnestly with both hands was for princes and judges to ask for a reward. This is from the word *shiloom*, and as Micah uses it, it means a bribe. So, princes and judges, people who were supposed to be impartially hearing matters and calling things fairly, no matter who was involved, were instead selling their decisions to the highest bidder.

This was a charge that most of the prophets, major and minor, leveled against the people.

The second step in all of the wicked men of Micah's day being able to do evil earnestly with both hands is found in the phrase *and the great man, he uttereth his mischievous desire.* This ties into the first part of the picture, the princes and judges asking for a reward, a bribe. The great man is the one doing the bribing; he tells them what wicked thing or decision he wants, they name the price for him to pay for them to rule in his favor, and he pays it.

The third and final step in all of the wicked men of Micah's day being able to do evil earnestly with both hands is found in the phrase *so they wrap it up.* "They" are the princes, judges, and great men involved in this pay-for-play scheme. For them to wrap it up means that they weave all of their desires together into a dirty threefold cord, impossible for the victims to break.

The depravity of the very best

Micah 7:4 *The best of them is as a brier: the most upright is sharper than a thorn hedge: the day of thy watchmen and thy visitation cometh; now shall be their perplexity.*

In any wicked land, you would well expect to find some who were not so far gone in their depravity. But as Micah looked out at Israel, the conclusion he came to was that *The best of them is as a brier* and *the most upright is sharper than a thorn hedge.*

Whoever would have been regarded as the best among them, Micah knew that he was just like a briar: too flimsy to build with, and quick to cut those who came into contact with him.

Whoever would have been regarded as the most upright among them, Micah knew that he was just like an entire thorn hedge; nothing good could ever come from any contact.

Because of this depth of depravity from the very best they had to offer, Micah said, *the day of thy watchmen and thy visitation cometh; now shall be their perplexity.* Long had the watchmen had little or nothing to do; now, they would be scrambling to sound all of the alarms as God's visitation, in the form of the Assyrian scourge, came swarming into the land.

They enjoyed their years of perversity; now would come the time of their perplexity, or as we would put it, their utter confusion and uncertainty of what to do.

The dishonor of the closest

Micah 7:5 *Trust ye not in a friend, put ye not confidence in a guide: keep the doors of thy mouth from her that lieth in thy bosom.* **6** *For the son dishonoureth the father, the daughter riseth up against her mother, the daughter in law against her mother in law; a man's enemies are the men of his own house.*

Jeremiah uttered a similar proclamation in his prophecy:

Jeremiah 9:4 *Take ye heed every one of his neighbour, and trust ye not in any brother: for every brother will utterly supplant, and every neighbour will walk with slanders.*

Jeremiah spoke of it as a coming state of being; Micah proclaims that it is now here. The days were so evil that a friend could not safely trust a friend or put any confidence in a guide, a close advisor, as we would put it, or even speak freely to his own wife as he lay holding her at night. Absolutely anyone would sell you out; you may as well have been all alone on an island.

Going further into this thought, Micah says *For the son dishonoureth the father, the daughter riseth up against her mother, the daughter in law against her mother in law; a man's enemies are the men of his own house.*

Four things are seen here, four more indications of just how bad things were. Sons were dishonoring their own fathers. Daughters were rising up against their mothers. Daughters-in-law were rising up against their mothers-in-law. A man's enemies were not found after he left the safety of his home; they were found within the very walls of his home.

Many years later, Jesus made reference to this when speaking of the coming days of persecution:

Matthew 10:21 *And the brother shall deliver up the brother to death, and the father the child: and the children shall rise up against their parents, and cause them to be put to death.*

To Micah, it was already a present-day reality.

The decision of the wise

What do you do when it seems as if everything is bad and no one can be trusted? Micah's decision was this:

Micah 7:7 *Therefore* [because no one can be counted on] *I will look unto the LORD; I will wait for the God of my salvation: my God will hear me.*

In reality, unlike in Micah's day, we normally have more people we can count on than we realize. And yet, it is never a bad plan to simply look to the LORD and wait for the God of our salvation, because He always hears us!

We may one day look around and honestly be able to say, along with Micah, "Where have all the good men gone?" But we will never be able to honestly say, "Where has my good God gone?" because He will always hear us. We may not see His face, we may not feel His hand, but we can always know that we have His ear.

Chapter Eight
In That Day

Micah 7:8 *Rejoice not against me, O mine enemy: when I
fall, I shall arise; when I sit in darkness, the LORD shall be a light
unto me.* **9** *I will bear the indignation of the LORD, because I have
sinned against him, until he plead my cause, and execute judgment
for me: he will bring me forth to the light, and I shall behold his
righteousness.* **10** *Then she that is mine enemy shall see it, and
shame shall cover her which said unto me, Where is the LORD thy
God? mine eyes shall behold her: now shall she be trodden down
as the mire of the streets.* **11** *In the day that thy walls are to be
built, in that day shall the decree be far removed.* **12** *In that day
also he shall come even to thee from Assyria, and from the fortified
cities, and from the fortress even to the river, and from sea to sea,
and from mountain to mountain.* **13** *Notwithstanding the land
shall be desolate because of them that dwell therein, for the fruit
of their doings.* **14** *Feed thy people with thy rod, the flock of thine
heritage, which dwell solitarily in the wood, in the midst of
Carmel: let them feed in Bashan and Gilead, as in the days of old.*
15 *According to the days of thy coming out of the land of Egypt
will I shew unto him marvellous things.* **16** *The nations shall see
and be confounded at all their might: they shall lay their hand
upon their mouth, their ears shall be deaf.* **17** *They shall lick the
dust like a serpent, they shall move out of their holes like worms
of the earth: they shall be afraid of the LORD our God, and shall
fear because of thee.* **18** *Who is a God like unto thee, that*

pardoneth iniquity, and passeth by the transgression of the remnant of his heritage? he retaineth not his anger for ever, because he delighteth in mercy. **19** *He will turn again, he will have compassion upon us; he will subdue our iniquities; and thou wilt cast all their sins into the depths of the sea.* **20** *Thou wilt perform the truth to Jacob, and the mercy to Abraham, which thou hast sworn unto our fathers from the days of old.*

In the first seven verses of Micah 7, Micah lamented that there were no good men to be found in the land. And, should God have chosen, that would certainly seem to be a fitting end to the book of Micah, which has been negative throughout.

But that was not God's choice at all. Yes, Israel would fall to Assyria, and Judah would fall to Babylon, but the story would not end there. There would come a day in which the God who allowed the last grains of sand to slip away from Israel's side of the hourglass turned it back over, brought her back, and instead allowed time to run out on Assyria and Babylon.

A decree for the enemy

Micah 7:8 *Rejoice not against me, O mine enemy: when I fall, I shall arise; when I sit in darkness, the LORD shall be a light unto me.*

As Micah's prophecy begins to draw to a close, the hourglass indeed begins to turn. Up until this point, there has been little to see of a positive nature; both Israel and Judah have sinned, both Israel and Judah must fall. But now, everything changes. Micah speaks as if for Judah and Israel, and addresses both Assyria and Babylon.

The decree is for that enemy in each case to refrain from rejoicing when Israel/Judah's fall finally came at their hands. Yes, they would fall, but they would also arise. Yes, they would for a long while sit in the darkness of captivity, but even there, the LORD would be a light to them.

This should tell us certain important things about our own day and about future days. Certain hideous trends seem to always find a way to become fashionable again. Recently, the mullet of replacement theology/anti-Semitism has once again become a very popular thing. But God has never, and will never, forsake His people, the Jews. Yes, they rejected His Son, but neither the Father nor the Son ever has or ever will stop loving them, nor will a single promise made to them ever go unfulfilled. They will be restored, they will be given the full breadth of their promised earthly kingdom. Further, they will finally come to know and embrace the Messiah that they have so long refused to acknowledge.

That being the case, each and every enemy of the Jews would be well advised to rethink their putrid, self-immolating position.

A dramatic turn of events

Micah 7:9 *I will bear the indignation* [za-aph, rage like a storm] *of the LORD, because I have sinned against him, until he plead my cause, and execute judgment for me: he will bring me forth to the light, and I shall behold his righteousness.*

Still speaking in place of his people, Micah acknowledges their sin and proclaims them as willing to bear the indignation God will put upon them as a result of that sin. They will bear that indignation *until he plead my cause, and execute judgment for me.* There would come a day, then, when God turned from pleading against them, as he described in Micah 6:2, to pleading for them as He describes here. The prosecutor would become the defender, and Assyria and Babylon, the rod of His judgment against His people, would instead become the targets of His judgment on behalf of His people.

Further, Micah proclaimed *he will bring me forth to the light, and I shall behold his righteousness.* No day would ever be so dark as the day they were marched away from their homeland into the pitch blackness of captivity; no day would ever be so bright as they day God brought them back to that land, and they finally beheld His righteousness, which had always been there for them to see the entire time, if only they had desired to behold it.

Micah 7:10 *Then she that is mine enemy shall see it, and shame shall cover her which said unto me, Where is the LORD thy God? mine eyes shall behold her: now shall she be trodden down as the mire of the streets.*

In this verse, Micah, under the inspiration of God, gave his people a view of the future, and us a view of the past. There came a day when God's people fell, and this particular fall, as further verses will show, refers to the fall of Judah at the hands of the Babylonians. When that happened, the Babylonians did not just defeat them; they denigrated them as well. They mocked them, saying, "So, where is your Jehovah, that supposedly all-powerful God of yours?"

They got that haughty attitude toward God from the top of their food chain, king Nebuchadnezzar himself:

Daniel 3:15 *Now if ye be ready that at what time ye hear the sound of the cornet, flute, harp, sackbut, psaltery, and dulcimer, and all kinds of musick, ye fall down and worship the image which I have made; well: but if ye worship not, ye shall be cast the same hour into the midst of a burning fiery furnace; and <u>who is that God that shall deliver you out of my hands?</u>*

Nebuchadnezzar's grandson, Belshazzar, similarly mocked Jehovah by drinking booze out of the sacred cups taken from the Temple in Jerusalem. So when Micah said *Then she that is mine enemy shall see it, and shame shall cover her which said unto me, Where is the LORD thy God?* and followed that with *mine eyes shall behold her: now shall she be trodden down as the mire of the streets,* it was a promise that God was one day going to say, "I'm right here, on my throne where I have always been, and now it is your turn to be wrecked."

That very thing happened while the booze was still glistening on the lips of Belshazzar. He was slain that very night, and the Medes and Persians took the kingdom.

Micah 7:11 *In the day that thy walls are to be built, in that day shall the decree be far removed.*

When Jerusalem fell for good in 586 BC, the walls of the city were destroyed:

2 Kings 25:10 *And all the army of the Chaldees, that were with the captain of the guard, brake down the walls of Jerusalem round about.*

In Nehemiah 2, King Artaxerxes of Persia issued the command for the rebuilding of the city and the wall under the hand of Nehemiah. In that day, the decree that Micah referenced in verse eleven, meaning the decree for the people to be wrecked and removed into captivity, was far removed, or "removed by an extreme length."

The measure of that length is not hard to figure out:

Psalm 103:12 *As far as the east is from the west, so far hath he removed our transgressions from us.*

The character of God is such that, when He removes something, He really does remove it. Judah would not have to live in fear of God changing His mind and sending them back into the captivity from whence He rescued them; in that day, the decree was indeed "far removed."

There would be even more of a positive nature to that day, though:

Micah 7:12 *In that day also he shall come even to thee from Assyria, and from the fortified cities, and from the fortress even to the river, and from sea to sea, and from mountain to mountain.*

You will find a great deal of debate among commentators as to who the *he* and the *thee* of verse twelve are. The two schools of thought both generally agree that the *thee* refers to the land of Israel, and that is abundantly clear from the context. As to the *he,* though, the division generally falls into two camps, the first of which believes it to refer to the Jews returning to their land, and the other of which believes it to refer to heathen nations coming up to the restored nation of Israel seeking their favor.

To me, this is really not a hard debate to settle. *That day* of verse twelve clearly refers directly back to *the day* of verse eleven, the day that the walls were rebuilt. That being the case, all it takes is a quick perusal of the book of Nehemiah to see that heathen nations definitely did not come flooding in seeking their favor; in fact, even those near around them quickly sought their destruction.

But you may rest assured that in that day, and in the short years that followed, dispersed Jews *from Assyria* [which had been absorbed by Babylon], *and from the fortified cities* [strongholds where they had been kept as slaves], *and from the fortress* [Matsor, a nickname for Egypt] *even to the river* [the Euphrates, a thousand miles to the East of Israel], *and from sea to sea, and from mountain to mountain* [seas in general and mountains in general] came home. By the time of Christ, a few hundred years later, the land was once again filled with them.

Micah 7:13 *Notwithstanding the land shall be desolate because of them that dwell therein, for the fruit of their doings.*

Micah just delivered to his people God's promise of a future restoration. Now, though, he brings them back to the present with an ominous "notwithstanding." His thought runs like this: "But even though you will be restored in the future, in the meantime, the land is going to be desolate because of you; this is the fruit of your doings, and you will reap what you have sown."

Micah 7:14 *Feed thy people with thy rod, the flock of thine heritage, which dwell solitarily in the wood, in the midst of Carmel: let them feed in Bashan and Gilead, as in the days of old.*

You need to understand the voices of verses fourteen and fifteen to accurately see the picture. It will be Micah speaking to God in verse fourteen, and God answering in verse fifteen.

Micah's first request to God is that He feed His people with His rod, people that he then describes as the flock of God's heritage. This pictures God as the Shepherd of His sheep, His people, leading them to pasture and tending to their every need.

Micah then describes the people as they *which dwell solitarily in the wood, in the midst of Carmel.* And while that may seem peaceful and quiet and wonderful to us, please remember that Micah was accurately describing the people as sheep. Sheep, alone in the woods, will not survive long at all. This is why Micah was asking God to once again be their Shepherd.

Micah closed the requests of verse fourteen by saying *let them feed in Bashan and Gilead, as in the days of old.* Bashan and Gilead were lush, well-watered spots in the land. So Micah was asking God to shepherd his people, and in the words of David from so many years before, make them lie down in green pastures and lead them beside the still waters.

Here is how God answered all of that:

Micah 7:15 *According to the days of thy* [Israel of the past] *coming out of the land of Egypt will I shew unto him* [Israel of the future] *marvellous things.*

After all of the doom and destruction God promised to level His people with, after the captivity He promised to subject them to, there were no words of future encouragement that could have been uttered that would be more welcome than these. Would they go into captivity? Yes; but they had been in captivity before, in Egypt. Would they be powerless to do anything about it? Yes, but they had been powerless in Egypt as well.

God promised to do mighty works against their future captors, Assyria and Babylon, that would rival His mighty works against their past captor, Egypt. And while He did not use the overt, unmistakable miracles He used in Egypt, the devastation on Assyria and Babylon actually exceeded that which fell upon Egypt.

Egypt survived and continues to exist to this day.

Assyria and Babylon quickly fell and are nothing more than archaeological digs in our day.

Micah 7:16 *The nations shall see and be confounded at all their might: they shall lay their hand upon their mouth, their ears shall be deaf.*

When the captors of Israel and Judah fell, they would experience a unique kind of shame. They would be confounded [*boosh*, put to shame] at their might, meaning at their own might. They would be proud and arrogant in how strong they were, vainly imagining that they could never be broken—and God would absolutely break them. It would be so bad that they would lay their hand on their mouth, which even to this day is a universal sign of overwhelming shock. Their ears would be deaf—not so much literally, as unwilling to hear what was happening all around them as they were wrecked and leveled.

Micah 7:17 *They shall lick the dust like a serpent, they shall move out of their holes like worms of the earth: they shall be afraid of the LORD our God, and shall fear because of thee.*

The description in this verse is as degrading as could ever be imagined in that day. For proud, arrogant men to be reduced to crawling on the ground with their faces in the dirt, as if they were snakes or worms, was the ultimate in humiliation. Worse still, they would do so because of their fear of the very Jehovah God they had so mocked, and the people of God that they had so long enslaved.

A starker turn of events would be hard to even imagine. Seeing this, and realizing the miracle that it represented, Micah was then compelled to ask God the obvious question:

Micah 7:18 *Who is a God like unto thee, that pardoneth iniquity, and passeth by the transgression of the remnant of his heritage? he retaineth not his anger for ever, because he delighteth in mercy.*

The question Micah asked expected a negative answer: no one, absolutely no one, is like Him. It is also a question that had been asked before in Israel's history, strikingly enough, after God rescued them from their first captivity in Egypt:

Exodus 15:11 *Who is like unto thee, O LORD, among the gods? who is like thee, glorious in holiness, fearful in praises, doing wonders?*

When Moses asked the question, he did so because of God's demonstrated power. When Micah asked it, he did so because of God's divine pardon, saying, *that pardoneth iniquity, and passeth by the transgression of the remnant of his heritage? he retaineth not his anger for ever, because he delighteth in mercy.*

Was Israel guilty? Yes. Could she undo a single wrong thing she had ever done? No. So instead, God granted her a pardon, a *nawsaw*, a lifting up and carrying away of their iniquity. He then went further and passed by, *awbar*, moved beyond the transgression of what was left of His heritage, the Children of Israel. In complete picture form, God picked their filthiness up off of them as if it were a burden on their backs, set it aside entirely, and then walked away from it.

Why would He do that? Because *he retaineth not his anger for ever, because he delighteth in mercy.* God in His holiness always gets angry at sin and always somchow punishes it. But, unlike mankind, He does not *stay* angry, because He delights in mercy. He *levels* judgment because it is the right thing to do, but He does not *like* judgment. What He likes is mercy, withholding the destruction that we truly deserve.

Micah 7:19 *He will turn again, he will have compassion upon us; he will subdue our iniquities; and thou wilt cast all their sins into the depths of the sea.*

There are four particulars and one unique change of direction in this singular verse. Speaking to the people, people who have been assured of their coming destruction and then have heard of a future restoration, Micah proclaims to them that God will *turn again*. He had turned away from them, and He will turn back to them.

Second, God will *have compassion upon us*. He had been bitterly angry against them, but His heart will turn to them again in tender affection.

Third, God will *subdue our iniquities*. The word used for subdue was pointed, picturesque, and perfect for the occasion. Subdue is from *kabash*, and it means to bring into bondage. God would send His people into bondage because of their iniquities but would later send their iniquities into bondage so they could be free.

And that brings us to the fourth item: God will *cast all their sins into the depths of the sea.* It is not just that God would forgive, it is that He would remove the sin itself far from them so that they did not have access to it and could not fall prey to it again.

That is exactly what happened. Idolatry, ever their downfall, was never an issue again after the seventy years of captivity in Babylon. The Baals and bulls and Molochs and Ashtoreths were bygone relics, never revered again by a people made wiser by long chastisement.

As to the change of direction, look at verse nineteen one more time:

Micah 7:19 ***He*** *will turn again,* ***he*** *will have compassion upon us;* ***he*** *will subdue our iniquities; and* ***thou*** *wilt cast all their sins into the depths of the sea.*

Do you see it in your mind? Looking at the people while pointing up to heaven, Micah says, ***He*** *will turn again,* ***he*** *will have compassion upon us;* ***he*** *will subdue our iniquities.* Then Micah looks up to heaven, points back at the people, and says, *and* ***thou*** *wilt cast all their sins into the depths of the sea.*

This was not an academic exercise to Micah; he felt it all to the depths of his soul.

Still looking up to heaven, Micah closed his prophecy thusly:

Micah 7:20 *Thou wilt perform the truth to Jacob, and the mercy to Abraham, which thou hast sworn unto our fathers from the days of old.*

God made Abraham, Isaac, Jacob, and the nation of Israel that came from them, an unconditional, everlasting covenant. They will always and forever be His people, as far as nations are concerned. They will never cease to exist. They will have a thousand years in which they enjoy the full breadth of the land promise made to them. And they will one day also become, along with the saved of all nations, His people spiritually. Many years later, Paul put it this way:

Romans 11:26 *And so all Israel shall be saved: as it is written, There shall come out of Sion the Deliverer, and shall turn away ungodliness from Jacob:* **27** *For this is my covenant unto them, when I shall take away their sins.*

Neither Assyria nor Babylon would ever have believed it. Both were utterly convinced that, as with so many nations they had devastated before them, the sands had slipped forever away out of Israel's hourglass.

As it turned out, though, the God of Israel was the one holding that hourglass, and in His good time, He would turn it, draining Assyria and Babylon away into a forgotten nothingness, and restoring His people in full measure.

Nahum

Chapter Nine
The Burden of Nineveh

Nahum 1:1 *The burden of Nineveh. The book of the vision*
of Nahum the Elkoshite. **2** *God is jealous, and the LORD*
revengeth; the LORD revengeth, and is furious; the LORD will
take vengeance on his adversaries, and he reserveth wrath for his
enemies. **3** *The LORD is slow to anger, and great in power, and*
will not at all acquit the wicked: the LORD hath his way in the
whirlwind and in the storm, and the clouds are the dust of his feet.
4 *He rebuketh the sea, and maketh it dry, and drieth up all the*
rivers: Bashan languisheth, and Carmel, and the flower of
Lebanon languisheth. **5** *The mountains quake at him, and the hills*
melt, and the earth is burned at his presence, yea, the world, and
all that dwell therein. **6** *Who can stand before his indignation?*
and who can abide in the fierceness of his anger? his fury is
poured out like fire, and the rocks are thrown down by him. **7** *The*
LORD is good, a strong hold in the day of trouble; and he knoweth
them that trust in him. **8** *But with an overrunning flood he will*
make an utter end of the place thereof, and darkness shall pursue
his enemies. **9** *What do ye imagine against the LORD? he will*
make an utter end: affliction shall not rise up the second time. **10**
For while they be folden together as thorns, and while they are
drunken as drunkards, they shall be devoured as stubble fully dry.
11 *There is one come out of thee, that imagineth evil against the*
LORD, a wicked counsellor. **12** *Thus saith the LORD; Though*
they be quiet, and likewise many, yet thus shall they be cut down,

when he shall pass through. Though I have afflicted thee, I will afflict thee no more. **13** *For now will I break his yoke from off thee, and will burst thy bonds in sunder.* **14** *And the LORD hath given a commandment concerning thee, that no more of thy name be sown: out of the house of thy gods will I cut off the graven image and the molten image: I will make thy grave; for thou art vile.* **15** *Behold upon the mountains the feet of him that bringeth good tidings, that publisheth peace! O Judah, keep thy solemn feasts, perform thy vows: for the wicked shall no more pass through thee; he is utterly cut off.*

The background of the prophet and prophecy

Nahum 1:1 *The burden of Nineveh. The book of the vision of Nahum the Elkoshite.*

When you come to the name Nineveh in the Minor Prophets, it is always Jonah that immediately comes to mind:

Jonah 1:1 *Now the word of the LORD came unto Jonah the son of Amittai, saying,* **2** *Arise, go to Nineveh, that great city, and cry against it; for their wickedness is come up before me.*

This was during the prosperous reign of Jeroboam the Second. Jonah already knew from the writing of Hosea that the Assyrians, with their great capital city of Nineveh, would one day come against Israel and utterly wreck them. So Jonah ran, not wanting them to repent, wanting them, in fact, to be destroyed.

We know how that story ended. Jonah, after God broke his stubborn will, went and preached in Nineveh, and everyone there repented before God.

Here is what you need to know, then, about the timing of the book of Nahum. Nahum was written a hundred and fifty years after Jonah. (Jamieson et al., 612)

The turning to God of Jonah's day did not last forever. At some point, Nineveh and all of Assyria returned to their wicked ways. Maybe it was one generation later, maybe two or three, but eventually, things fell into place for the prophecy of Hosea to come to be. And that was not all on Assyria; it would be nice to blame them entirely, but as we saw throughout Micah's prophecy, it was Israel's sin and rebellion against God that brought the Assyrian scourge down on them anyway. As to the obvious Jonah question, then, was he right in how he viewed the call to go to Nineveh, seeing as how Nineveh did ultimately come against Israel as he feared, and then against Judah as well?

Certainly not. The entire city of Nineveh in his day repented before God—likely some two million people. When Jonah got to Paradise and then, later on, to Heaven, he found a countless multitude of Assyrians there, redeemed and rejoicing in the God of Israel! As the book of Nahum opens, though, we read of a very different circumstance. Here it is once again:

Nahum 1:1 *The burden of Nineveh. The book of the vision of Nahum the Elkoshite.*

Nahum is prophesying of the burden on Nineveh. This burden does not indicate a sadness of heart, as we often use it in our day. It is from the word *mawsaw*, and it means an exaction, a tax, a price laid on someone. God was calling the debt of Nineveh due; they had wrecked His people, Israel, before the days of Nahum, and were attempting to do the same to Judah. Instead, God would turn the hourglass and wreck them.

As to Nahum himself, not only is this the only book of the Bible in which he is mentioned, verse one is the only verse in the Bible in which he is mentioned. And all that we are told of him in this singular verse is his name, which means "comfort," and that he was an Elkoshite, likely meaning that he was a native of Elkoshai, a small village of Galilee. (Clarke, 730)

We do know, from verse fifteen of chapter one, that though he spoke many words applicable to the now-fallen Northern Kingdom of Israel, he prophesied most directly to Judah.

The bearing of the LORD

Nahum 1:2 *God is jealous, and the LORD revengeth; the LORD revengeth, and is furious; the LORD will take vengeance on his adversaries, and he reserveth* [nawtar, maintains, keeps] *wrath for his enemies.*

Jealous, revengeth, revengeth, furious, vengeance, adversaries, wrath, enemies. If you get the sense from verse two that God was about to utterly unleash on Assyria, your sense is correct.

Both instances of revengeth and the singular usage of vengeance are from the word *naqam*. As in our language, it means punishment and retribution for a wrong that has been done.

God was jealous over His people. Yes, He used Assyria to punish them for their wickedness, but that did not make the Assyrians righteous. What they did to Israel was horrific; what they attempted to do to Judah was as well, and they were about to find themselves the targets of Israel and Judah's very jealous God.

In the words *adversaries* and *enemies,* we find that God is simply not okay with everyone. And the people He has always been at greatest odds with are those who come against His people, the Jews; if you are an enemy of the Jews, you are an enemy of God and will be treated as such.

Nahum 1:3 *The LORD is slow to anger, and great in power, and will not at all acquit the wicked: the LORD hath his way in the whirlwind and in the storm, and the clouds are the dust of his feet.*

After verse two, in which we see that God is a furious God, the assurance of verse three that He is *slow to anger* bears some examination. Is God furious? Does He reserve wrath for His enemies? Yes, beyond a doubt. But remember, God gave Assyria a space of one hundred fifty years between the days of Jonah and the prophecy of Nahum. Yes, God gets bitterly angry, but He does not do so as we do, instantly flying off the handle. Here is how Peter expressed that many centuries later:

2 Peter 3:9 *The Lord is not slack concerning his promise, as some men count slackness; but is longsuffering to us-ward, not willing that any should perish, but that all should come to repentance.*

Here is how Ezekiel expressed the same thing:

Ezekiel 33:11 *Say unto them, As I live, saith the Lord GOD, I have no pleasure in the death of the wicked; but that the wicked turn from his way and live: turn ye, turn ye from your evil ways; for why will ye die, O house of Israel?*

Man may come to judgment, but he will always wade through the longsuffering and patience of the LORD on his way there.

Verse three continues, though, with the assurance that God is *great in power, and will not at all acquit the wicked: the LORD hath his way in the whirlwind and in the storm, and the clouds are the dust of his feet.*

God's patience is often mistaken for weakness. That is and will always be a fatal mistake, for God has none of that. Nor will He ever acquit [*naqah*, declare as innocent] the wicked. Assyria may have viewed herself as pure, but God certainly did not.

When Nahum proclaimed that the LORD *hath his way in the whirlwind and in the storm, and the clouds are the dust of his feet*, it could be viewed as God stirring up a whirlwind (tornado) and storm of judgment. The context of Nahum itself, though, leads me to view this whirlwind and storm as the actions of Assyria herself. She wreaked havoc on Israel and tried to do so in Judah. She was as destructive as a tornado. And yet, God had His way in all of it. The dust it stirred up was under His feet, not over His head.

Continuing the thought of God's power, Micah then says this of Him:

Nahum 1:4 *He rebuketh the sea, and maketh it dry, and drieth up all the rivers: Bashan languisheth, and Carmel, and the flower of Lebanon languisheth.* **5** *The mountains quake at him,* *and the hills melt, and the earth is burned at his presence, yea, the world, and all that dwell therein.*

Nahum now continues with his majestic description of God by showing His power over creation. The first two phrases seem to allude back to His parting and drying of the Red Sea and the Jordan River. When Assyria got this message from Nahum, they would doubtless remember the account of those things; everyone in that part of the world did.

The second descriptive set is that *Bashan languisheth, and Carmel, and the flower of Lebanon languisheth.*

Bashan, Carmel, and the prime parts of Lebanon are described as languishing under the judgment of God. Those were the most fruitful regions of the land; for them to languish would take a mighty God indeed.

In verse five's description, *The mountains quake at him, and the hills melt, and the earth is burned at his presence, yea, the world, and all that dwell therein,* we find, not a reminder of God's great dealings in the past, but a reference to His promised judgments of the future. The fulfilment of these words is seen at length in the book of the Revelation, and in summary in the writings of Peter:

2 Peter 3:10 *But the day of the Lord will come as a thief in the night; in the which the heavens shall pass away with a great noise, and the elements shall melt with fervent heat, the earth also and the works that are therein shall be burned up.*

Assyria, then, was being warned that they had gloried over the wrong people, because Israel/Judah's God was not like any other God.

Seeing all of this, Nahum asked the logical questions:

Nahum 1:6 *Who can stand before his indignation? and who can abide in the fierceness of his anger? his fury is poured out like fire, and the rocks are thrown down by him.*

The expected answer to these questions was "No one; absolutely no one." If Lucifer himself, second only in power to

God, was helpless before Him, no one at all has the power to stand before His indignation ["za-am," rage] and no one at all can abide ["koom," stand upright in the presence of] the fierceness of His anger.

Assyria would further read that *his fury is poured out like fire, and the rocks are thrown down by him.* They would learn the hard way that such was indeed the case. Their destruction would be complete and permanent.

The next two verses will paint a contrast between how God deals with His own and His enemies:

Nahum 1:7 *The LORD is good, a strong hold in the day of trouble; and he knoweth them that trust in him.* **8** *But with an overrunning flood he will make an utter end of the place thereof, and darkness shall pursue his enemies.*

In the first verse, see Israel and Judah. In the second verse, see Assyria. In a wider sense, in the first verse, see everyone who ever trusts in God, and in the second, see anyone who ever determines to fight against those who trust in God.

Yes, in the waning days of the kingdom, neither Israel nor Judah could hardly have been accused of trusting in God. But for most of their history, they did, and there would come a day when they would do so again. Their stronghold of their land would be taken; their stronghold of the LORD would ever remain.

As for Assyria, though, her fate would be much different. Nahum said, *But with an overrunning flood he* [the LORD] *will make an utter end of the place thereof* [Nineveh], *and darkness shall pursue his enemies.*

There is a pointed prophecy in these words. God promised to end Nineveh with an overrruning flood; those were not symbolic words.

There is a reference in ancient history (though its accuracy is debated) to Sardanapalus of Assyria. A coalition of Medes and Babylonians rebelled against them. The walls were strong, though, and it very much seemed like Nineveh would withstand the rebellion.

A siege was laid. It went long and did not seem at all like it was going to succeed. But in the third year of the siege, the rains came in torrents. The Tigris River flooded so violently that a large section of the wall was toppled and washed away.

Sardanapulus, seeing that Nineveh was likely to fall, built a huge funeral pyre in the palace, locked himself and his wives in, and burned everyone and everything to the ground. (Lenormant & Chevallier)

If all of this is correct, Assyria survived and rebuilt, barely, but in a greatly weakened condition. Their respite would not be long; twenty years or so later, we know for certain that they fell for good to the Medo-Babylonians.

The Babylonians seem to have learned from that account and used a similar tactic in the final destruction of Nineveh in 612 BC. Assyria's walls were thick and high—they were also made of sun-dried clay bricks, which would have been very susceptible to water, especially a strong river redirected at its foundation.

God was angry with Assyria, and about forty years after the prophecy of Nahum, they would learn the hard way what that meant.

The bemusement of the situation

Nahum 1:9 *What do ye imagine against the LORD? he will make an utter end: affliction shall not rise up the second time.*

The question, evincing mock confusion, is directed from Nahum to the Assyrians. We have a Biblical record of what they "imagined against the LORD:"

2 Kings 18:35 *Who are they among all the gods of the countries, that have delivered their country out of mine hand, that the LORD should deliver Jerusalem out of mine hand?*

Rabshakeh of Assyria uttered these mocking words. And yet, Nahum said, *he* [the LORD] *will make an utter end: affliction shall not rise up the second time.* This means that when the promised destruction from the LORD came upon them, there would not need to be a second.

History has proven that evaluation to be correct.

Nahum 1:10 *For while they be folden together as thorns, and while they are drunken as drunkards, they shall be devoured as stubble fully dry.*

The picture presented in this verse is dripping with power. The people of Assyria are pictured as a bunch of thorns all tangled together. People generally do not want to get anywhere near that; you will do little but get cut and bleed.

They had a problem, though. Like many in the ancient world, they were sodden drunks. And while they were drunk in their palaces, the forces of Babylon would come against them, and do the most sensible thing with matted thorns: they would simply burn them to the ground.

Nahum 1:11 *There is one come out of thee, that imagineth evil against the LORD, a wicked counsellor.*

There are several candidates for the identity of the individual spoken of in this verse. We have already seen Rabshakah, but this could also easily apply to Sennacharib or many others. Regardless of who it was, there was an Assyrian who qualified as a wicked counselor.

The word for wicked is one any regular reader of Scripture will almost certainly be familiar with: *belial*. It means worthless, a good-for-nothing, and it is often used as a description of children of the devil. Assyria would have one of these whipping his people up against the LORD, and against the people of the LORD.

It would not go well for those who followed his counsel:

Nahum 1:12 *Thus saith the LORD; Though they be quiet, and likewise many, yet thus shall they be cut down, when he shall pass through. Though I have afflicted thee, I will afflict thee no more.*

God is speaking of the Assyrians in the first half of the verse and to His people in the second half of the verse. Of the Assyrians, God noted that though they be quiet, meaning un-threatened and un-bothered, and though they be many in number, they would be cut down when he, meaning the Babylonians He commissioned against them, passed through.

To His people, Judah, though, God said, *Though I have afflicted thee, I will afflict thee no more.* Assyria would be broken by Babylon and never again be a threat to Judah.

Nahum 1:13 *For now will I break his yoke from off thee, and will burst thy bonds in sunder.*

For a long time, Judah had been reduced to paying tribute to Assyria as a condition for being allowed to exist:

2 Kings 18:14 *And Hezekiah king of Judah sent to the king of Assyria to Lachish, saying, I have offended; return from me: that which thou puttest on me will I bear. And the king of Assyria appointed unto Hezekiah king of Judah three hundred talents of silver and thirty talents of gold.*

Assyria would continue to oppress Judah like this and in other ways until God Himself put everything to a stop. God did indeed break the Assyrian bonds from off of Judah; Judah still lives, Assyria has been gone for nearly three millennia.

Nahum 1:14 *And the LORD hath given a commandment concerning thee, that no more of thy name be sown: out of the house of thy gods will I cut off the graven image and the molten image: I will make thy grave; for thou art vile.*

All of verse fourteen seems most properly to apply to Assyria. God gave a commandment concerning them that their name would no more be sown. In other words, it would no more be carried all over the world. That fearsome people, constantly on everyone's whispering lips, would cease to be spoken of. Further, God would visit her house of idols and cut off her graven and molten images.

All of that has been done. People pretty much never speak of Assyria anymore unless teaching about them from the Bible, and her idols and images are now nothing more than historical footnotes.

Most ominously, though, God went on to say, *I will make thy grave; for thou art vile.* It means exactly what it sounds like; God so loathed the sight and sounds of Assyria that He said, in so many words, "Here, let me make a nice grave to bury you in."

When God decides to make a grave for you, you know you have messed up as badly as is humanly possible.

The beauty of good tidings

Nahum 1:15 *Behold upon the mountains the feet of him that bringeth good tidings, that publisheth peace! O Judah, keep thy solemn feasts, perform thy vows: for the wicked shall no more pass through thee; he is utterly cut off.*

If these words sound familiar, it is because you know them from a different book of the Bible, where they are applied a bit of a different way:

Romans 10:15 *And how shall they preach, except they be sent? as it is written, How beautiful are the feet of them that preach the gospel of peace, and bring glad tidings of good things!*

In Paul's day, he was applying the words of Nahum to spiritual salvation. When Nahum wrote them, though, he, like Isaiah's nearly identical words of Isaiah 52:7, was applying them to the coming salvation from the Assyrian scourge. Anyone bringing that message of salvation would indeed be regarded as bringing a beautiful message on beautiful feet.

Closing out the first chapter of his prophecy, Nahum then addressed Judah directly, saying, *O Judah, keep thy solemn feasts, perform thy vows: for the wicked shall no more pass through thee; he is utterly cut off.*

The point of those words was to tell them to go ahead and worship as if nothing at all was wrong, because God was about to make it where nothing at all was wrong.

Judah was carrying a burden borne of circumstances. Assyria was carrying a very different kind of burden, one borne of corruption.

Judah's burden would be removed, and Judah would forever remain. Assyria would be removed, and her burden would forever remain.

Chapter Ten
When The Emptiers Are Emptied

Nahum 2:1 *He that dasheth in pieces is come up before thy face: keep the munition, watch the way, make thy loins strong, fortify thy power mightily.* **2** *For the LORD hath turned away the excellency of Jacob, as the excellency of Israel: for the emptiers have emptied them out, and marred their vine branches.* **3** *The shield of his mighty men is made red, the valiant men are in scarlet: the chariots shall be with flaming torches in the day of his preparation, and the fir trees shall be terribly shaken.* **4** *The chariots shall rage in the streets, they shall justle one against another in the broad ways: they shall seem like torches, they shall run like the lightnings.* **5** *He shall recount his worthies: they shall stumble in their walk; they shall make haste to the wall thereof, and the defence shall be prepared.* **6** *The gates of the rivers shall be opened, and the palace shall be dissolved.* **7** *And Huzzab shall be led away captive, she shall be brought up, and her maids shall lead her as with the voice of doves, tabering upon their breasts.* **8** *But Nineveh is of old like a pool of water: yet they shall flee away. Stand, stand, shall they cry; but none shall look back.* **9** *Take ye the spoil of silver, take the spoil of gold: for there is none end of the store and glory out of all the pleasant furniture.* **10** *She is empty, and void, and waste: and the heart melteth, and the knees smite together, and much pain is in all loins, and the faces of them all gather blackness.* **11** *Where is the dwelling of the lions, and the feedingplace of the young lions, where the lion, even the old lion,* *walked, and the lion's whelp, and none made them afraid?* **12** *The lion did tear in pieces enough for his whelps, and strangled for his lionesses, and filled his holes with prey, and his dens with ravin.* **13** *Behold, I am against thee, saith the LORD of hosts, and I will burn her chariots in the smoke, and the sword shall devour thy young lions: and I will cut off thy prey from the earth, and the voice of thy messengers shall no more be heard.*

In chapter one of Nahum, God called the payment due for the deeds of Ninevah, the capital city of Assyria. God used Assyria to judge Israel, taking her into captivity, and He allowed Assyria to come against Judah and do much harm there.

But that did not make the deeds of Assyria right. They were, in fact, evil to the core, and they delighted in that evil.

God commissioned Nahum to declare their coming judgment at the hands of the Babylonians.

Nahum will continue doing so in chapter two.

A hopeless instruction

Nahum 2:1 *He that dasheth in pieces is come up before thy face: keep the munition, watch the way, make thy loins strong, fortify thy power mightily.*

As Nahum utters these words, he still has an eye to the future. Specifically, he is once again looking ahead in time to the coming destruction of the Assyrian Empire at the hands of the Medo-Babylonians. It is that growing empire, the Medo-Babylonians, that the pronoun *he* refers to in verse one, rather than just to a singular person.

This empire that will topple Assyria is described as *He that dasheth in pieces*. Interestingly, this is the only time the Old Testament that this Hebrew word, *puwts*, is translated this way. Most of the time, it simply means to scatter. Here, though, forseeing the violence that was about to be leveled upon Assyria, scattering was not nearly a strong enough word or term. They were not merely going to be chased out of their land; they were going to be beaten into a million pieces right there within their land.

In the face of this coming devastation, God gave Assyria four instructions that under normal cases would have been helpful instructions, but in this case was intentionally a set of hopeless instructions. Those instructions were that they *keep the munition, watch the way, make thy loins strong,* and *fortify thy power mightily*.

Keep the munitions meant to guard the strongholds. They were not to simply trust their walls or gates; they were to have men stationed upon them.

Watch the way meant that they were to have lookouts watching far down the road so they could have as much advanced warning as possible about the coming enemy armies.

Make thy loins strong was a euphemistic way of saying that they were to take courage, be manly, be valiant.

Fortify thy power mightily meant that they were to be at maximum capacity both in manpower and in weapons.

All of these instructions that God was giving to the Assyrians were logical, sensible instructions. People who would do these things would seem to stand a chance. And yet, God was not giving Assyria these instructions to give them a chance; He was giving them these instructions because they did not have a chance. This was anger wrapped in irony, and the next verse explains why:

Nahum 2:2 *For the LORD hath turned away the excellency of Jacob* [put here for Judah, the Southern Kingdom], *as the excellency of Israel: for the emptiers have emptied them out, and marred their vine branches.*

God was going to destroy Assyria because Assyria had destroyed Israel and had attempted the destruction of Judah. Yes, He Himself had allowed them to come against His people, but that did not change the fact that what they did was wicked and wrong, and they reveled in every moment of it.

Assyria is described here as emptiers who emptied Israel out and marred their vine branches. That description is fitting; they deported such masses from the North that it forever ceased to be a kingdom. They then imported others from foreign lands as replacements, with disastrous results:

2 Kings 17:24 *And the king of Assyria brought men from Babylon, and from Cuthah, and from Ava, and from Hamath, and from Sepharvaim, and placed them in the cities of Samaria instead of the children of Israel: and they possessed Samaria, and dwelt in the cities thereof.* **25** *And so it was at the beginning of their dwelling there, that they feared not the LORD: therefore the LORD sent lions among them, which slew some of them.* **26** *Wherefore they spake to the king of Assyria, saying, The nations which thou hast removed, and placed in the cities of Samaria, know not the manner of the God of the land: therefore he hath sent lions among them, and, behold, they slay them, because they know not the manner of the God of the land.*

Assyria emptied and marred Israel. God would return the favor, and no preparations she would make to stop it would make the slightest difference.

A horrific incursion

Nahum 2:3 *The shield of his mighty men is made red, the valiant men are in scarlet: the chariots shall be with flaming torches in the day of his preparation, and the fir trees shall be terribly shaken.*

The Babylonians were especially fond of red and habitually made their shields appear red, either through the use of copper or paint. (Feinberg, 194) This gave a fearsome appearance to the people who were seeing them coming. As verse three informs us, all of her valiant men would also be dressed in scarlet red, a very deep crimson, when they attacked Assyria.

The chariots would be equipped with flaming torches, which would both heighten the horror, and serve as a handy way to burn everything to the ground. And there would be so many chariots that the fir trees would shake from the rumbling of all the wheels.

Nahum 2:4 *The chariots shall rage in the streets, they shall justle one against another in the broad ways: they shall seem like torches, they shall run like the lightnings.*

Nahum gives us a fine bit of personification in verse four. The chariots of the Babylonians would make their way to the very streets of Nineveh, and every other major place in the Assyrian Empire as well. When they did, it would not be for a tour; they would be raging in the streets. It would be as if the chariots themselves were violently angry and determined to wreak havoc on the enemy.

The chariots would justle, or as we would say in our vernacular, jostle one against another. The significance of that is that it would be happening in the broad ways; this would not be a matter of narrow streets, it would be a matter of overwhelming numbers of chariots on the streets.

The two final bits of descriptions that Nahum gives here are that *they shall seem like torches, they shall run like the lightnings*. The chariots would be outfitted with torches, and thus, would seem like rolling torches themselves. They would be going so fast that it would seem to the terrified victims as if they were moving like lightning.

Nahum 2:5 *He shall recount his worthies: they shall stumble in their walk; they shall make haste to the wall thereof, and the defence shall be prepared.*

Verse five begins to open our insight as to what would be happening with the king of Assyria when all of this took place. He, the king of Assyria, would *recount his worthies* in the face of all this; in other words, he would go down the list of all of his mightiest men and hurry them to the walls and gates to defend against this attack. It would all be so hurried and unbelievable, though, that these mighty men would stumble in their walk; they would be falling all over themselves trying to get the walls and gates rather than proceeding in an orderly fashion. Nonetheless, they would hurry to the wall, and they would prepare their best defense against the imminent Babylonian scourge.

Nahum 2:6 *The gates of the rivers shall be opened, and the palace shall be dissolved.*

It is at this point that a bit of historical background will be very eye-opening. We have been referring to the Medo-Babylonian Empire that formed to come against Asyria. Ironically, it would later be an alliance of the Medes and the Persians that turned and came against Babylon.

This Medo-Babylonian alliance was formed between Cyaxares of the Medes and Nabopolassar of the Babylonians. Nabopolassar was the father of a son who would become far more famous than himself: Nebuchadnezzar.

Here is the description that Feinberg gave of how everything played out:

> "Cyaraxes surrounded the city on the north. During the early assaults of the invading armies, the Ninevites inflicted heavy losses on the besieging forces. To celebrate these initial successes the Assyrians gave themselves over to carousings and revelings. The besiegers took advantage of the situation and drove the Assyrians behind their walls. A part of the Assyrian troops were put to flight and driven into the Tigris River. The city itself remain safe.
>
> "In the *third year of the siege, however, heavy rains brought on a flood which broke down the walls about the city. This is exactly the picture given by the prophet. The canals of the great Tigris were opened and the palace was destroyed." (Feinberg, 195) *(Some historians have the siege lasting just three months rather than three years.)

Thus, as we have previously mentioned, both natural and man-made flooding were used in the destruction of Nineveh.

Nahum 2:7 *And Huzzab shall be led away captive, she shall be brought up, and her maids shall lead her as with the voice of doves, tabering upon their breasts.*

This is the only verse in the Bible that the name Huzzab is found. And, as with so many instances in the minor prophets, we will quickly find that it is more of a nickname that a proper name, a declaration rather than a designation. Huzzab is from the word *natsab*, which means to take a stand. In the context of Nahum 2, it clearly refers to Assyria. They were the ones who had taken a stand and, yet, had fallen anyway and would be led into captivity.

The description of her being led away into captivity is poetic. It says, *she shall be brought up, and her maids shall lead her as with the voice of doves, tabering upon their breasts.*

Assyria is pictured as a royal lady whose maidens are having to lead her to her fate. They are cooing like doves, trying to get her to put one trembling foot in front of the other. At the same time, they are beating on their breasts like they are drums, for that is what the word *tabering* means.

Nahum 2:8 *But Nineveh is of old like a pool of water: yet they shall flee away. Stand, stand, shall they cry; but none shall look back.*

When Nahum said that *Nineveh is of old like a pool of water*, he was speaking literally, not euphemistically. The river wall of Nineveh on the Tigris was 4530 yards long. Dams around the city formed a water barricade. (Feinberg, 195)

All of this should have afforded her ample security. Yet in spite of that fact, Nahum proclaimed *yet they shall flee away. Stand, stand, shall they* [the military leaders] *cry* [to their soldiers]*; but none shall look back.* This was going to be a complete and utter rout, and on the home field.

Nahum 2:9 *Take ye the spoil of silver, take the spoil of gold: for there is none end of the store and glory out of all the pleasant furniture.*

This was God's command to the invading Babylonians. Just like the Assyrians emptied out the treasures of Israel, the Babylonians would return the favor and empty out the treasures of Assyria. As it turns out, what goes around really does come around.

Nahum 2:10 *She is empty, and void, and waste: and the heart melteth, and the knees smite together, and much pain is in all loins, and the faces of them all gather blackness.*

Verse ten gives us a three-part description followed by a four-part description. The initial and simple three-part description of Assyria at her fall is that *She is empty, and void, and waste.* These words are synonyms by nature; each one is designed to paint the picture of hollow wreckage. Jamieson, Fausset, and Brown put it this way: "Literally, 'emptiness, and emptiedness, and devastation.' The accumulation of substantives without a verb (as in Na 3:2), the two first of the three being derivatives of the same root, and like in sound, and the number of syllables in them increasing in a kind of climax, intensify the gloomy effectiveness of the expression." (Jamieson et al., 618)

Gloomy effectiveness is a good way to describe it. The more detailed four-part description that follows, each phrase starting with the word and, is *and the heart melteth, and the knees smite together, and much pain is in all loins, and the faces of them all gather blackness.*

The first two describe the reactions of utterly terrified people. The second two describe people in horrific pain. The terror of the earth was falling, and they were now on the other side of the paradigm than the side with which they were so long familiar.

A haunting inquiry

Nahum 2:11 *Where is the dwelling of the lions, and the feedingplace of the young lions, where the lion, even the old lion, walked, and the lion's whelp, and none made them afraid?*

It should not escape your notice that there are five mentions of lions in this one singular verse. No creature in Scripture was used as consistently as a symbol of strength and power as the lion. The Assyrians themselves frequently used sculptures and carvings of lions on just about everything.

This question, then, from God through the mouth of His prophet, was designed as a taunt. He wanted to know where all of the brave lions were that the world had so long feared? Could this really be that place, the city where the bravest of men were running and screaming in terror and abandoning their posts?

The subject of lions will still be in view in verse twelve:

Nahum 2:12 *The lion did tear in pieces enough for his whelps, and strangled for his lionesses, and filled his holes with prey, and his dens with ravin.*

I love Adam Clarke's picturesque take on this verse. He said of it, "This verse gives us a striking picture of the manner in which the Assyrian conquests and depredations were carried on. How many people were spoiled to enrich his whelps-his sons, princes, and nobles! How many women were stripped and slain, whose spoils went to decorate his lionesses-his queen, concubines, and mistresses. And they had even more than they could assume; their holes and dens-treasure-houses, palaces, and wardrobes-were filled with ravin, the riches which they got by the plunder of towns, families, and individuals." (Clarke, 736)

They truly had seemed unstoppable. They had conquered and slain and stolen as if they were and would always be the only lions on the plain. Unfortunately for them, they drew the notice and the ire of a Lion far higher than themselves:

Nahum 2:13 *Behold, I am against thee, saith the LORD of hosts, and I will burn her chariots in the smoke, and the sword* *shall devour thy young lions: and I will cut off thy prey from the earth, and the voice of thy messengers shall no more be heard.*

The battle was over from the moment Jehovah God said *I am against thee.* Especially given that He then described Himself as the Lord of hosts, meaning the Lord of armies, His intention and the outcome were never in doubt. He would destroy Assyria's chariots, kill her young, strong soldiers (lions) with the sword, and cut off her prey, starving her of sustenance.

Finally, though, He added, *and the voice of thy messengers shall no more be heard.* Why would He end with that? Let's go back in time, just a bit, and the answer will not be too hard to find:

2 Kings 18:28 *Then Rabshakeh stood and cried with a loud voice in the Jews' language, and spake, saying, Hear the word of the great king, the king of Assyria:* **29** *Thus saith the king, Let not Hezekiah deceive you: for he shall not be able to deliver you out of his hand:* **30** *Neither let Hezekiah make you trust in the LORD, saying, The LORD will surely deliver us, and this city shall not be delivered into the hand of the king of Assyria.* **31** *Hearken not to Hezekiah: for thus saith the king of Assyria, Make an agreement with me by a present, and come out to me, and then eat ye every man of his own vine, and every one of his fig tree, and drink ye every one the waters of his cistern:* **32** *Until I come and take you away to a land like your own land, a land of corn and wine, a land of bread and vineyards, a land of oil olive and of honey, that ye may live, and not die: and hearken not unto Hezekiah, when he persuadeth you, saying, The LORD will deliver us.* **33** *Hath any of the gods of the nations delivered at all his land out of the hand of the king of Assyria?* **34** *Where are the gods of Hamath, and of Arpad? where are the gods of Sepharvaim, Hena, and Ivah? have they delivered Samaria out of mine hand?* **35** *Who are they among all the gods of the countries, that have delivered their country out of mine hand, that the LORD should deliver Jerusalem out of mine hand?*

God clearly never forgot that messenger of Assyria, nor the challenge he uttered. But there came a day when it wasn't a messenger asking where God was, but God asking where all of the messengers were.

Truly, the emptiers became the emptied.

Chapter Eleven
Incurable

Nahum 3:1 *Woe to the bloody city! it is all full of lies and robbery; the prey departeth not;* **2** *The noise of a whip, and the noise of the rattling of the wheels, and of the pransing horses, and of the jumping chariots.* **3** *The horseman lifteth up both the bright sword and the glittering spear: and there is a multitude of slain, and a great number of carcases; and there is none end of their corpses; they stumble upon their corpses:* **4** *Because of the multitude of the whoredoms of the wellfavoured harlot, the mistress of witchcrafts, that selleth nations through her whoredoms, and families through her witchcrafts.* **5** *Behold, I am against thee, saith the LORD of hosts; and I will discover thy skirts upon thy face, and I will shew the nations thy nakedness, and the kingdoms thy shame.* **6** *And I will cast abominable filth upon thee, and make thee vile, and will set thee as a gazingstock.* **7** *And it shall come to pass, that all they that look upon thee shall flee from thee, and say, Nineveh is laid waste: who will bemoan her? whence shall I seek comforters for thee?* **8** *Art thou better than populous No, that was situate among the rivers, that had the waters round about it, whose rampart was the sea, and her wall was from the sea?* **9** *Ethiopia and Egypt were her strength, and it was infinite; Put and Lubim were thy helpers.* **10** *Yet was she carried away, she went into captivity: her young children also were dashed in pieces at the top of all the streets: and they cast lots for her honourable men, and all her great men were bound in* *chains.* **11** *Thou also shalt be drunken: thou shalt be hid, thou also shalt seek strength because of the enemy.* **12** *All thy strong holds shall be like fig trees with the firstripe figs: if they be shaken, they shall even fall into the mouth of the eater.* **13** *Behold, thy people in the midst of thee are women: the gates of thy land shall be set wide open unto thine enemies: the fire shall devour thy bars.* **14** *Draw thee waters for the siege, fortify thy strong holds: go into clay, and tread the morter, make strong the brickkiln.* **15** *There shall the fire devour thee; the sword shall cut thee off, it shall eat thee up like the cankerworm: make thyself many as the cankerworm, make thyself many as the locusts.* **16** *Thou hast multiplied thy merchants above the stars of heaven: the cankerworm spoileth, and flieth away.* **17** *Thy crowned are as the locusts, and thy captains as the great grasshoppers, which camp in the hedges in the cold day, but when the sun ariseth they flee away, and their place is not known where they are.* **18** *Thy shepherds slumber, O king of Assyria: thy nobles shall dwell in the dust: thy people is scattered upon the mountains, and no man gathereth them.* **19** *There is no healing of thy bruise; thy wound is grievous: all that hear the bruit of thee shall clap the hands over thee: for upon whom hath not thy wickedness passed continually?*

Nahum has spent two chapters thus far utterly excoriating Assyria. Bear in mind, that, as he was doing so, Assyria seemed invincible. And yet, Nahum prophesied of her soon-coming destruction in terms as certain as if it had already happened.

He will continue to do so until the very last verse of the book.

The woe

Nahum 3:1 *Woe to the bloody city! it is all full of lies and robbery; the prey departeth not;*

By now, the identity of the bloody city is not at all in question. Nineveh has already been named as the subject of the book in 1:1, 2:8, and will be named as such again in 3:7.

Nineveh, capital of Assyria, was indeed a bloody city. Even by the brutal standards of the ancient world, it was beyond the pale. Further, it was also a city filled with lies and robbery, and a city where no prey was ever released. Little wonder, then, that in the utter lack of truth, respect for property, and mercy for people, God pronounced a woe upon them, an expression of coming doom.

Nahum 3:2 *The noise of a whip, and the noise of the rattling of the wheels, and of the pransing* [dahar, galloping] *horses, and of the jumping chariots.* **3** *The horseman lifteth up both the bright sword and the glittering spear: and there is a multitude of slain, and a great number of carcases; and there is none end of their corpses; they stumble upon their corpses:*

These verses once again give us a vivid description of the coming Medo-Babylonian alliance and what it would do to Nineveh. The city that had been untouchable and absolutely at ease would suddenly find itself invaded. The noise of cracking whips would ring out in every street and from every corner. The deafening roar of countless chariot wheels, and rushing horse hooves, and chariots that were coming off the ground and landing hard back down on it would not be able to be drowned out.

Horsemen would be holding bright swords and glittering spears up to catch the sun, before bringing them down on their terrified Assyrian victims.

There would be so many dead bodies that they could not be counted. Those still alive would be tripping over the slain as they tried to run and save themselves.

The whoredoms and witchcraft

Nahum 3:4 *Because of the multitude of the whoredoms of the wellfavoured harlot, the mistress of witchcrafts, that selleth nations through her whoredoms, and families through her witchcrafts.*

The *because* that begins verse four looks backward, not forward. It refers to all of the woe and judgment God prescribed against Nineveh in the first three verses.

So, what was the cause?

There were two stated in verse four, one in the first and third phrase, the other in the second and fourth phrase.

The first charge is *the multitude of the whoredoms of the wellfavoured harlot* and *that selleth nations through her whoredoms*. The Assyrians were a sexually promiscuous, openly debauched people.

The second charge is *the mistress of witchcrafts* and *that selleth nations ...through her witchcrafts.* The Assyrians were a deeply occultic people and were drawing other nations into their dark worship.

God would deal with her according to her sin:

Nahum 3:5 *Behold, I am against thee, saith the LORD of hosts; and I will discover thy skirts upon thy face, and I will shew the nations thy nakedness, and the kingdoms thy shame.* **6** *And I will cast abominable filth upon thee, and make thee vile, and will set thee as a gazingstock.*

Ominously, God now says the same thing in verse five that He said just five verses earlier at the end of chapter two, *Behold, I am against thee, saith the LORD of hosts*. Did Assyria have a great army and great walls? Certainly. Would they be any match for Jehovah God, the God of armies? Absolutely not.

In judgment of her whoredoms, God said *and I will discover thy skirts upon thy face, and I will shew the nations thy nakedness, and the kingdoms thy shame.* This refers to the ancient practice of humiliating caught prostitutes by stripping them naked and covering their faces with their clothing as they were paraded publicly through the streets. God was going to humiliate Assyria in the most degrading way possible.

In judgment of her witchcraft, God said *And I will cast abominable filth upon thee, and make thee vile, and will set thee as a gazingstock.* As with people who committed infamous crimes and were then put into public stocks for people to come by and throw mud and filth upon them, so Assyria would be degraded and embarrassed.

God has always been very serious and very exact about the law of sowing and reaping.

The waste

Nahum 3:7 *And it shall come to pass, that all they that look upon thee shall flee from thee, and say, Nineveh is laid waste: who will bemoan her? whence shall I seek comforters for thee?*

In Nahum's day, anyone looking on Nineveh would have done so with wonder and admiration. But when the promised judgment fell, everyone that looked on her would run like rats from a sinking ship. As they ran, they would have one statement and two questions falling off their lips.

The statement would be *Nineveh is laid waste.* That is from the word *shadad*, and it means to violently destroy, to utterly wreck and ruin. The questions would be *who will bemoan her?* and *whence shall I seek comforters for thee?*

Those questions were not spoken out of concern; they were spoken as a mockery. They were an indication that none would bemoan her, meaning that none would lament her fall, and that even if comforters were to be sought, none would ever be found.

Assyria became the powerhouse of the earth by being utterly ruthless and cruel and showing not a shred of mercy to anyone. Thus, when it came her time to fall, she would find no one shedding a tear at her demise.

People who have never shown mercy cannot rightly expect mercy to be shown to them.

Assyria was doubtless made aware of the prophecy of Nahum; such things did not go unnoticed in the ancient world. And when they heard of their coming destruction, they no doubt scoffed; there was no power on the horizon that could ever seem to knock them off of their lofty perch. That is what God had in mind by the question He then posed to them:

Nahum 3:8 *Art thou better than populous No, that was situate among the rivers, that had the waters round about it, whose rampart was the sea, and her wall was from the sea?* **9** *Ethiopia and Egypt were her strength, and it was infinite; Put and Lubim were thy helpers.*

As I previously mentioned, Assyria was surrounded by water, and thus had a position that should have been impregnable. But, had they merely looked to history, they would have found that they were not the first people so situated, and that things did not end well for their forerunners. As Feinberg observes:

> No, meaning No Amon (also called Thebes), "was the great capital of Upper Egypt. Students of Egyptian history consider it the first great city of the Near East, describing its ruins as the most magnificent of any ancient civilization anywhere in the world. It was the capital city of the Pharaohs of the Eighteenth to the Twentieth Dynasties.
>
> "It was located on both banks of the River Nile. Homer, the first Greek poet, spoke of it as having 100 gates. Its ruins cover an area of some 27 miles."
>
> Further, No Amon was even better off than Nineveh, for the former had strong allies (Ethiopia, Egypt, Put, Lubim, v. 9), whereas the latter had alienated all the nations about her. And yet, in spite of all this, she suffered defeat and captivity. She was captured by Sargon of Assyria in his campaign against Egypt. (Feinberg, p. 199)

Here was God's point in that historical reference, a reference that they themselves should have no trouble understanding since they participated in No's fall:

Nahum 3:10 *Yet was she carried away, she went into captivity: her young children also were dashed in pieces at the top of all the streets: and they cast lots for her honourable men, and all her great men were bound in chains.*

No fell. Assyria would fall. No went into captivity, Assyria would go into captivity. The citizens of No saw their young children smashed to the ground in the top of all the streets; Assyria would see the same thing. No saw all of her great men gambled for and sold into slavery, bound with chains and carried away, and Assyria would suffer the same fate.

Nahum 3:11 *Thou also shalt be drunken: thou shalt be hid, thou also shalt seek strength because of the enemy.*

When the Medo-Babylonian Empire came against them and when it was evident that they would fall, the citizens of Assyria would turn to the bottle and try to drink away their horror. They would hide rather than fight. They would seek for strength from some ally, because the enemy was too great for them.

Nahum 3:12 *All thy strong holds shall be like fig trees with the firstripe figs: if they be shaken, they shall even fall into the mouth of the eater.*

The word picture Nahum painted here was stark. When the first ripe figs of a tree were ready, the least shake of the branch would send them crashing to the ground. In like manner, ripe with all of her wickedness, the least shaking of the approaching army against them would cause them to fall and be devoured by the eater, Medo-Babylon.

The women

Nahum 3:13 *Behold, thy people in the midst of thee are women: the gates of thy land shall be set wide open unto thine enemies: the fire shall devour thy bars.*

There is an insult worth examining in this verse. God, through Nahum, told Assyria *Behold, thy people in the midst of thee are women.* The reason this was an insult is because he was talking about the men; he was talking about the soldiers, their finest warriors. For a woman to be called a woman is not an insult; they are the lovely and precious creatures God created them to be. For a man to be called a woman always has been and always will be an insult, and every man knows it. The finest men that Assyria had to offer were being described as if they were in dresses and running screaming through the streets trying to hide from the big, strong enemy that was bearing down on them.

Little wonder, then, that the next thing we read is *the gates of thy land shall be set wide open unto thine enemies: the fire shall devour thy bars.* When men cease to be manly, when they cease to be strong and powerful and brave and willing to fight, a land will not stand, no matter how high their walls or how advanced their technological fighting machines. This is exactly why the devil and his family have spent so many years in America trying to feminize men. It is exactly why they have spent so long uttering ridiculous phrases like "toxic masculinity" and trying to get men to be little more than bigger versions of women.

Remove the warriors, ruin a nation.

The wound

Nahum 3:14 *Draw thee waters for the siege, fortify thy strong holds: go into clay, and tread the morter, make strong the brickkiln.*

As in the first verse of chapter two, the words given here are a hopeless instruction. This is God mocking Assyria by telling them exactly what they need to do to prepare for the approaching enemy. It is God giving them wise words that will not help, because their destruction is already assured.

The first instruction He gives them is to draw waters for the siege. They are to make sure that they have enough water stored up within the city to outlast the armies that will camp around them.

The second instruction is that they are to fortify the strong holds. As before, this means to fully man all of the walls and the gates, put soldiers on them, and not just rely on the walls and gates themselves.

The third instruction is that they are to *go into clay, and tread the morter, make strong the brickkiln*. This means that they were to make bricks and mortar and have them ready to repair damage that would be done each day to the wall by the enemies outside who were trying to get in. And yet, in that last instruction, we find their destruction:

Nahum 3:15 *There* [in the brick kiln where you are making bricks] *shall the fire devour thee; the sword shall cut thee off, it shall eat thee up like the cankerworm: make thyself many as the cankerworm, make thyself many as the locusts.*

In the place where they were using fire to make bricks to protect themselves, the fire would instead devour them. Their trowels would not help; the sword would cut them off. It, the enemy with his sword and fire, would cut them off. They had been as numerous as locusts, and yet they would be destroyed as if locusts had descended upon them.

Nahum 3:16 *Thou hast multiplied thy merchants above the stars of heaven: the cankerworm spoileth, and flieth away.* **17** *Thy crowned are as the locusts, and thy captains as the great grasshoppers, which camp in the hedges in the cold day, but when the sun ariseth they flee away, and their place is not known where they are.*

Assyria was not just famous for war; she was equally famous for commerce. All of the earth sought to her as a source of wealth. And yet, like the cankerworm phase of the locust, when destruction came upon them, all the merchants would fly away, leaving her to her fate.

Continuing the allusion of locusts, verse seventeen describes Assyria's own royal family and captains of the military, who were as numerous as grasshoppers, as crowned, yet cowardly.

When the sun arose on the day that it was clear the enemy would win, they would flee away and leave others to their fate.

And they were not the only ones:

Nahum 3:18 *Thy shepherds slumber, O king of Assyria: thy nobles shall dwell in the dust: thy people is scattered upon the mountains, and no man gathereth them.*

The shepherds refer to the rulers and tributary princes, who, as Herodotus informs us, deserted Nineveh in the day of her distress. (Clarke, 738) They were asleep at the helm when they should have been leading.

In the face of this utter vacuum of leadership, when Assyria fell, the people would be *scattered upon the mountains, and no man gathereth them.*

If all seemed hopeless, that is because it was:

Nahum 3:19 *There is no healing of thy bruise; thy wound is grievous: all that hear the bruit* [shema, the report] *of thee shall clap the hands over thee: for upon whom hath not thy wickedness passed continually?*

When we think of the word bruise in our language, we normally think of a mere skin contusion. But this word is much more serious than that. It is from the word *sheber*, and it means a crushing fracture. If you can picture someone being run over by large piece of equipment, that would be similar to the meaning of this word for bruise.

There would be no healing for what was wrong with Assyria. Her wound would be grievous; fatal, in fact. Everyone who heard of what had happened would clap their hands over Assyria, celebrating their fall, because her wickedness had always landed on everyone around her.

It did not seem possible. None of it seemed possible in the days of Nahum. I love the way Adam Clarke described the unlikeliness of all of it:

"What probability was there that the capital city of a great kingdom, a city which was sixty miles in compass, a city which contained so many thousand inhabitants, a city which had walls a hundred feet high, and so thick that three chariots could go abreast upon them, and which had one thousand five hundred towers, of two hundred feet in height; what probability was there that such a city should ever be totally destroyed? And yet so totally was it destroyed that the place is hardly known where it was situated." (Clarke, 739)

And all of it, all of this destruction of that mighty empire, started with the fact that they came against God's people and ravaged them.

Any man, any group, any nation that harbors anti-Semitism in their heart is holding tightly to their own assured destruction.

Works Cited

Clarke, A. (n.d.). Adam Clarke's commentary practical and explanatory on the whole Bible (Vol. 4). Abingdon-Cokesbury Press.

Feinberg, C. L. (1976). The Minor Prophets. Moody Press.

Henry, M. (1935). Matthew Henry's Commentary on the Whole Bible (Vol. 4). Fleming H. Revell.

Jamieson, R., Fausset, A. R., & Brown, D. (1997). A Commentary on the Old and New Testaments (Vol. 2). Hendrickson Publishers.

Keil, C. F., & Delitzsch, F. (1967). Biblical Commentary on the Old Testament: The Twelve Minor Prophets (Vol. 1). WM. B. Eerdmans Publishing Company.

Lenormant, F., & Chevallier, E. (2012, June 30). About. History Moments. https://historyweblog.com/2012/06/destruction-of-assyria/

Socher, A. (2024, February 1). *Offended by the apostle paul (02.01.24)*. Plain Bible Teaching. https://plainbibleteaching.com/podcast/020124/

Wagner, B. (2025). Joel, Amos, Obadiah: Turmoil Among the Nations. Word of His Mouth Publishers.

Other Books by Pastor Bo Wagner

Colossians: The Treasures of Deity
Daniel: Breathtaking
Ephesians: The Treasures of Family
Esther: Five Feasts and the Fingerprints of God
Galatians: Treasures of Liberty
Hosea: Love When It Matters Most
James: The Pen and the Plumb Line
Joel, Amos, Obadiah: Turmoil Among the Nations
Jonah: A Story of Greatness
Nehemiah: A Labor of Love
Philippians: The Treasures of Joy
Proverbs Vol 1: Bright Light from Dark Sayings
Proverbs Vol 2: Bright Light from Dark Sayings
The Revelation: Ready or Not
Romans: Salvation from A-Z
Ruth: Diamonds in the Darkness

Beyond the Colored Coat
From Footers to Finish Nails
Learning Not to Fear the Old Testament
Marriage Makers/Marriage Breakers
I'm Saved! Now What???
Don't Muzzle the Ox
Why Christmas?

Books in the Night Heroes Series

Cry from the Coal Mine (Vol 1)
Free Fall (Vol 2)
Broken Brotherhood (Vol 3)

The Blade of Black Crow (Vol 4)
Ghost Ship (Vol 5)
When Serpents Rise (Vol 6)
Moth Man (Vol 7)
Runaway (Vol 8)
Terror by Day (Vol 9)
Winter Wolf (Vol 10)
Desert Heat (Vol 11)
Deadline (Vol 12)
The Sword and the Iron Curtain (Vol 13)
Escape From Beaver Island (Vol 14)

Other Fiction

Zak Blue: Falcon Wing
Zak Blue: Enter the Maelstrom

Devotionals

DO Drops Vol. 1
DO Drops Vol. 2
DO Drops Vol. 3
DO Drops Vol. 4
DO Drops Vol. 5
DO Drops Vol. 6
DO Drops Vol. 7
DO Drops Vol. 8
DO Drops Vol. 9
DO Drops Vol 10
DO Drops Vol 11
DO Drops Vol 12
DO Drops Vol 13

www.ingramcontent.com/pod-product-compliance
Lightning Source LLC
LaVergne TN
LVHW010102110826
845155LV00028B/445

* 9 7 8 1 9 4 1 0 3 9 6 7 0 *